Prayer Changes People

Contents

Foreword

God is saying much to His Church about prayer today. In many parts of the world the Church is growing rapidly compared to the experience of the Church in Western Europe. The difference, many observe, is prayer. In Third World countries vast numbers of Christians know how to pray. But the Church in Europe still needs to learn from the life of Jesus and from the experience of those God is teaching personally. Books like this will help our understanding, and, please God, help to prod us into an ever deeper relationship with God in prayer.

I believe God is calling *every member* of His church to a ministry of prayer. For too long it has been regarded as the ministry of the specialists. When God's people begin to seek Him in earnest, then things will begin to change. And so will people. Prayer changes us before it changes others.

Christ's kingdom came in power, not so much when He preached, nor when He healed, but when He prayed. Our praying will bring us into line with God's will, so that He can work in power. It also will challenge the powers of darkness all around, as well as in the heavenly realms.

We need prayer warriors to release from Satan's grip areas of society, families and – dare I say it – the Church. Then the preachers, bringing God's word of truth by proclamation or by prophecy, will see abundant results.

I welcome this book and pray that it will help to fulfil these hopes in the life of every reader.

Some books or articles I have read have made a lasting impression on me. Words placed together in succinct fashion, or statements that have potency because of who said them as well as what they conveyed. Pithy, powerful pronouncements on prayer have particularly struck me and have found their way into my 'notes, quotes and anecdotes' file. Sometimes, however, a preacher or author can produce sermons, articles or even books that are distilled equivalents of what others have said. Originality and freshness therefore suffer.

Michael Cole in this book has maintained a very good balance. Quotable quotes there are in abundance – some his own, some from other sources – but this is no dry replica of other writings. It has his own style and experience.

There are many books which are experience-oriented; some make exciting and captivating reading. Autobiographical detail can however place authors on a pedestal and make them remote from their fellow mortals. Other books speak about every one else's experience, but their substance is remote from the author's own reality.

Michael Cole blends together his experience as a vicar, a family man, the leader of Mission to London's Prayer Committee, and his interest in South America. He draws sensitively from the real-life situations of others and himself to show how prayer works. The chapters on Praise, Confession and Intercession ring with truth related to his own experience.

The Bible is sometimes taught in theological terms, which stretches and satisfies the intellectual, but is beyond the uninitiated. At other times the Bible is used merely as a resource book for anecdotes.

Michael Cole avoids both extremes. His teaching on prayer is thoroughly Biblical; it has substance without being heavy.

I also welcome the opportunity of writing this Foreword, especially as both Michael Cole and I have been writing a book on prayer at the same time. We share the same longing – to see a people of prayer and a people of power, bringing glory to our God and His Christ. And we hope in the process to throw a little more light on how that is possible.

Brian Mills, Prayer and Revival Secretary,
Evangelical Alliance, Reading, November, 1985.

Preface

What did 1984 mean to you? For some, throughout the world, it conjured up images of George Orwell – his book, and his prophecy of doom. For others, especially in England, it meant great evangelistic opportunities with Mission England and Mission to London. Thousands came forward to receive Christ, and to start a new life of faith in Jesus. It was the year of hope and good news.

In London, the Mission might not have taken place. All the plans were made, publicity was out, committees had been working hard, counsellors trained, the choir recruited, the money was coming in – all was under way, with one exception. Official permission to use the Stadium of Queens Park Rangers Football Club in West London had not yet been granted. Permission to use the arena depended upon a vital meeting of the local Council. The environmental health officers were concerned about the noise levels from the meetings, the possible disturbance to the neighbours and the problems to local traffic caused by hundreds of coaches and cars arriving and leaving each night. They had made their reports and the debate in the Council seemed to be going against the Mission.

Nearby in a local church a few key workers of the Mission were praying. At the same time the deputy director for Mission to London was in the public gallery of the Council chamber, and every now and then slipped out. With the help of a two-way walkie-talkie he kept those in the prayer meeting informed about the debate. They prayed, asking the Lord to overrule the Council.

When the vote was taken, four of the Council members were in favour, three against and one abstained. The Council granted permission. The Mission went ahead. We had seen God overruling in the affairs of men.

Towards the end of that same year, we had reached a point in our local church life where we needed a fresh vision of the work God wanted us to do. After prayer and discussion the church leaders decided to set aside a 'Week for Prayer' early in 1985. This time was to be a turning point for the church. I shall relate some of the events later in the book. Sufficient to say at this stage that God insisted on being made Head of His church, He showed us attitudes to be changed, He clarified the aims we should be fulfilling as a church – 'To know Christ and to make Him known' – and He indicated the next steps we should take.

Prayer – we believe – changed the voting in the London Borough Council. Prayer changed hearts and attitudes in our own church. I shall also share with you ways in which prayer has been answered over a very short period of time following a near fatal road accident, and over a much longer period of time for healing for a friend in a Karachi hospital. You can discover the full stories later in the book.

Now, if you protest that all this is pure coincidence, and you can't prove that prayer changes people, I will reply to you in two ways.

Firstly, I will remind you of the answer Archbishop William Temple gave to a doubter, who asked a similar question. 'When I pray, coincidences happen, and when I stop praying, coincidences stop happening.'

Secondly, I will share with you very briefly what prayer has meant in our personal lives, marriage and ministry. I suppose most men learn a lot about the Lord and prayer from their wives. That is true for me. The story begins more than ten years ago, when we were living and working in Manchester. We were privileged to work in a very famous and well attended church – Holy Trinity, Platt. The church was bursting with young people – students from the universities and colleges, as well as some lovely people from the Coronation Street-type parish area. Outwardly all was success and blessing, but inwardly we were both spiritually dry. My wife, Stephanie, had reached the point where, if the Christian life was a matter of doing this and running that, then she seriously wondered about giving it all up. For me, I was beginning to see the Christian ministry rather like walking around a large field, with a high hedge beyond which I could not see. Every year I walked around the festivals of the church, and I wasn't sure that I wanted to do this for another twenty years.

God has a way of breaking into such desperate situations. We had actually moved to a parish near London – where we are still working – and I was out of the country at the time. As Chairman of the South American Missionary Society I was able to visit most of the work in Latin America in which the mission was involved. What I did not know at the time was that on the morning I was due to fly home to Gatwick, Stephanie had reached a point where she knew the only thing she could do was to ask a lovely Christian mum in the congregation to pray for her that she might know the release and baptism of the Spirit. I was to come to a similar point more slowly a few months later. I had taken many years to get to that point. I needed to work my way through all the teaching in the New Testament about the gifts and ministries of the Holy Spirit to make sure they were available for today! I could not submit to anything that I did not find true to Scripture. Again, because I am the Vicar I did not find it easy to admit that I had a need, and the hardest thing to do was to pick up the 'phone and ask if I might go to someone who would pray for me.

The Holy Spirit released a whole new desire for dimension in, and discovery of prayer for us both. I was to learn a great deal through Stephanie – and really without her, this book would not have been written. She was to introduce me to some of the classics on prayer, and to the work of a fellowship like the Lydia Fellowship. Whereas before 1977 prayer had sometimes been a dull and dry duty that really didn't mean very much, now it was usually a daily delight. Beforehand a few minutes prayer seemed to last ages; now a few hours were not really long enough to have spiritual fellowship with the Lord Jesus. A whole new revolution took place in our personal lives that had various spin-offs in our marriage, which, I trust, have affected and influenced our children and others. At least, our children are now happy to enlist the help of the 'God squad' from time to time!

The Spirit changed us, and we now find that prayer is changing people.

Another milestone in my spiritual pilgrimage was the granting to me of some Sabbatical leave early in 1984. I was able to read widely on prayer, and also visit such areas of the world as America, Singapore, Australia and New Zealand and to discover more about the work God is doing. I came back with much more to share.

One way in which I was able to do this arose through 'Friday Focus'. For two or three years now, a number of ladies from various churches and fellowships in the area have met together for Bible teaching on a Friday morning. We have an Autumn and Spring term and a very short post-Easter session. Much of what I am sharing in this book first saw life in those teaching sessions. In those times, we were able to test and to earth much of what the Bible has to say about prayer. I am very grateful to two members of Friday Focus – Pamela Evans and Monica Mattock – for reading the manuscript and making many, very helpful, suggestions for improvement. I am grateful to Jackie Arnold, my secretary, for typing the manuscript – twice – a true labour of love, and I am indebted to Joan Hicks (whom we all know as Jix), a friend, a retired infant headmistress and indefatigable Christian worker – a young seventy year old – for other helpful suggestions.

If it is asked, 'Why another book on prayer?' I can only share with you my hopes for this book. Some of the Christian classics are still around and widely read, but often their style and language doesn't ring true to the 1980s. There are lots of books available that specialise in one aspect of prayer, such as praise or intercession; there are good introductory books but they somehow don't bring out the marvellous biblical teaching we have about the foundation for prayer found in the Trinity – Father, Son and Holy Spirit – nor make clear that in the spiritual battle we have to deal with the world, the flesh and the devil. I was looking for a general book on prayer, that would reveal the strong biblical basis for it, that would introduce us to some of the other great writings on prayer, earth it all in daily living and call us to embark upon a life and ministry of prayer both personally and in our churches. I couldn't find the book I was looking for, so I was encouraged by Edward England to write it! Whether I have succeeded, you must judge. I send it out with the constant prayer that God will be glorified and His people edified wherever they may be, throughout the world.

All biblical quotations are from the New International Version, unless otherwise stated.

Michael Cole
July 1985

One: Prayer – The Deciding Factor

Prayer is the deciding factor. In his *Quiet Talks on Prayer*, S. D. Gordon wrote:

> 'In its simplest meaning prayer has to do with a conflict. Rightly understood it is the deciding factor in a spiritual conflict. The scene of the conflict is the earth. The purpose of the conflict is to decide the control of the earth and its inhabitants.'[1]

In this opening chapter, I want to illustrate for you how prayer is, or was, the deciding factor in the life of the Lord Jesus, in the spiritual battle that every Christian faces, in the mission and task of the church, for the welfare of our society today, in the life of the church, in everyday life for us personally, as well as in the family.

In the life of Jesus

It is Luke who tells us most about Jesus' prayer life. Without going into great detail, we know that Jesus probably prayed every day (Mark 1.35 and Mark 6.46); he prayed when life was very busy and He was under pressure (Matthew 4.23 and Luke 5.15–16); He prayed when He was facing the crises of life and had very important choices to make (Luke 3.21–22, 6.12–13, 9.18, 21–22, 9.29, 22.39–46 and 23.46). Jesus prayed as a matter of habit during the course of His ministry (Luke 5.15, 11.1, John 12.27 and Mark 6.46), and He also prayed when faced with hunger, healing or death, situations that required a special manifestation of His power (Mark 1.35; 6.41, 7.34 and John 11.41).

This pattern of prayer was like a strand running through Christ's life. It was the theme dominating the whole symphony of His life; the very spiritual life blood of His relationship with His heavenly Father.

Prayer is the Christian's vital breath,
The Christian's native air,
His watchword at the gate of death:
He enters heaven with prayer.
(James Montgomery)[2]

Prayer must be that for us, because prayer was that for Jesus.

Prayer was also the means by which Jesus, tired from the extraordinary demands of people and their lives upon Him, found refreshment and renewal. It was the source of His inspiration that enabled Him to keep going, especially when His friends deserted Him, and the Cross stood before Him. Prayer was the means by which Jesus received His guidance as He discerned the will of His Heavenly Father. It was the channel through which flowed His praise and thanksgiving to God for His blessing. Prayer was the weapon Jesus used to prevent Satan getting a foothold in the lives of others, and victory over Himself, whether in the wilderness temptations or the agony in the Garden of Gethsemane. (Luke 4.42, 6.12, 9.28, 10.2, 10.21, 22.31–32, 22.39–40).

Writing about the prayer-life of Christ, J. Oswald Sanders said:

'It is true that only small fragments of the Master's life are preserved for us in the Gospels, but a large field may be seen through a small chink in the fence. The prayers of His that are recorded give us a rich insight into their character and material for our emulation. . . . From the records it would appear that of all His characteristics, the prayerfulness of Christ impressed His disciples most deeply. They did not ask Him to teach them how to preach or heal or teach, but they did make a request which each of us could take on our lips at this moment "Lord, teach us to pray" '.[3]

The excellence of Jesus' prayer life has been well contrasted with the poverty of our own. 'What a contrast between Christ's whole nights of prayer, His sustained seasons of sacred communion with the Father, on the one hand and the haste, the coldness, the thoughtlessness, and the selfishness that characterises our prayers, on the other'.[4] For Jesus, prayer was the deciding factor in His ministry.

In the spiritual battle

Sooner or later, we shall discover that the Christian is involved in a spiritual battle. The actual battle may be fought over the spread of the gospel, over some moral issue affecting the welfare of society, over some temptation we face in our own Christian living, or some area of our family life. Prayer will be the deciding factor in that battle.

Paul reminds the Ephesian Christians of the principles involved: 'Our struggle is not against flesh and blood, but against the rulers, against the authorities, against the power of this dark world, and against the spiritual forces of evil in the heavenly realms. Therefore put on the full armour of God . . . and pray in the Spirit on all occasions' (Eph. 5.12, 13 and 18).

There is a very clear illustration of this truth in the life of Moses. We are told (in Exodus 17) that the Amalekites attacked the Israelites at Rephidim. Joshua and his men fought against them down in the valley, while Moses, with Aaron and Hur, went to the top of the hill. 'As long as Moses held up his hands (in prayer), the Israelites were winning, but whenever he lowered his hands, the Amalekites were winning. When Moses' hands grew tired, they took a stone and put it under him and he sat on it. Aaron and Hur held his hands up – one on one side, one on the other – so that his hands remained steady till sunset. So Joshua overcame the Amalekite army with the sword' (Exod. 17.11–13).

Prayer didn't by-pass the use of the sword and human effort, but it complemented them. Prayer was the decisive factor in the battle and the future welfare of the Israelites. Thus, 'The greatest thing anyone can do for God and for man is to pray'.[5]

One very remarkable illustration of victory in the spiritual battle concerns a man called Sundar Singh. He was a missionary on the Tibetan border. On one occasion, by order of the chief lama, Singh was thrown into a dry well, the lid of which was then securely locked. He was accused of preaching the gospel in the market place.

Here he was left to die, like many others before him, whose bones and rotting flesh lay at the bottom of the well. On the third night, when he had been crying to God in prayer, he heard someone unlocking the lid of the well and removing it, and then a voice spoke, telling him to take hold of the rope which was being lowered. He was glad to find a loop at the bottom of the rope in which he could place his foot, for his right arm had been injured. He was then drawn up, the lid replaced and locked, but when he looked around to thank his rescuer he could find no trace of him. The fresh air revived him and his injured arm felt whole again. When morning came he returned to the city where he had been arrested and resumed preaching. News reached the lama that the man who had been thrown into the well for preaching had been liberated and was preaching again. Sundar Singh was brought before him, and told the story of his release. The lama declared that someone must have obtained the key and let him out, but when the search was made for the key it was found attached to the lama's own belt!

In the mission of the Church

The spiritual health and well-being of the home and overseas missionary work of the church so often reflect and reveal the spiritual and prayer life of the local and home church. Each generation needs to discover the promises of God's word that prayer is the deciding factor in:–

(a) *The provision of workers* Jesus teaches us that prayer is the crucial factor in the provision of workers, whether on the mission field, or for the ordained ministry of the church, or for the ministry and needs of each local church and fellowship: 'When Jesus saw the crowds, He had compassion on them, because they were harassed and helpless, like sheep without a shepherd. Then He said to His disciples, "The harvest is plentiful, but the workers are few. Ask the Lord of the harvest, therefore, to send out workers into His harvest field" ' (Matthew 9.36–38).

(b) *The preaching of the gospel* Despite all his natural abilities, great experience and intellectual powers, Paul still depended totally upon the Lord in his preaching and evangelistic ministry. He was not too proud to ask younger Christians to pray for him in this responsibility, thereby enrolling them as fellow labourers:

> 'And pray for us, too, that God may open a door for our message, so that we may proclaim the mystery of Christ, for which I am in chains. Pray that I may proclaim it clearly, as I should' (Col. 4.3–4).

As Dr Billy Graham has put it, there are three secrets to any effective evangelistic crusade. Number one – prayer. Number two – prayer. Number three – prayer. Prayer is to lead to increased evangelism in our lives and in our land.

(c) *The protection of the missionary* Protection is just as vital for the missionary in the twentieth century as it was in Paul's day, although travel conditions are very different: jet aircraft rather than Roman chariot. But in some areas of the jungle the way through is still by horseback or on foot. There is still the need to pray for protection from accidents, fatal diseases, human opposition, sudden heart attacks, and the tragedies of life from which the Christian is not promised exemption. No wonder Paul asked for prayer: 'Finally, brethren, pray for us that the message of the Lord may spread rapidly and be honoured, just as it was with you. And pray that we may be delivered from wicked and evil men, for not everyone has faith. But the Lord is faithful, and He will strengthen and protect you from the evil one' (2 Thess. 3.1–3). Or, as a returning missionary put it to his home church – 'Your kneeling keeps us standing.' One missionary, writing in his prayer letters, says: 'Thank you for your prayers for our safety from snakes and poisonous spiders. We've had examples of both even amongst the children's toys . . . God *really does* hear your prayers, so pray on. Secondly, to be translating Romans 5 means that since the last prayer-letter, we've done a complete check of Mark, distributed 1–3 John to the Mataco Reading Committee, and started working again through Romans. The work steams ahead. Thank you again.'[6]

(d) *The peace of the world* The modern missionary carries on the work in many different social and political contexts – be it a democratically elected government, or a Marxist dictatorship. There may be peace and harmony, there may be deep civil strife and tension. So the church, and especially the men, are called upon to pray for all those in authority: 'I urge . . . that requests, prayers, intercession and thanksgiving be made for everyone – for kings, and all those in authority, that we may live peaceful and quiet lives in all godliness and holiness' (1 Tim. 2.1–2). The reason for this instruction is that there may be peace and holiness and the opportunity for people to come to a knowledge of the truth.

Prayer is the deciding factor in the faithful and effective world-wide mission of the church. As Andrew Murray writes: 'Prayer is indeed a power on which the ingathering of the harvest and the coming of the kingdom do in very truth depend.'[7]

Dr R. A. Torrey reminds us that when praying for world mission we must pray for the workers, for men and women who have already gone overseas, for the outpouring of the Holy Spirit, for the national churches and leaders, for the home committees and officials and for the supply of money.[8]

I can personally testify that the prayers of Christians make a powerful difference. Whenever we have a specially important council meeting I seek the prayers of friends for the meeting, and time and again the Lord has given us His wisdom and guidance, in a way that we would not have anticipated.

For the welfare of society

The Christian – whoever he is – is called upon to submit to, honour and pray for those in authority, both at local and national level. (Rom. 13.1; 1 Pet. 2.16–17 and 1 Tim. 2.1). It is worth remembering that among those in authority when these words were written numbered men like the Emperor Nero. Jesus himself would have died as a baby had not God overruled the plans of Herod. In this twentieth century how might you have prayed if you were a Christian in pre-war Germany under Adolf Hitler, or in Uganda when Idi Amin was President? I believe that Scripture would have encouraged us to submit to them in all things lawful, honest and in line with God's will. But we can pray for evil to be restrained, and that those in authority will be removed from office. So long as they are in power we submit and honour, but we pray for the shortening of their time in office and the reduction of the wickedness they are allowed to perpetuate.

Most of us are not called upon to live in such

conditions as these, but in a moderate and calm society. It is, however, an increasingly secular, materialistic and godless society, in which God's authoritative standards are virtually ignored, and the rule of compromise and tolerance goes. For this reason there is just as great a need today for the Christian Church to pray for the leaders of the nations, the monarch or president, the judiciary, police force, leaders of industry and unions; also for the framers of public opinion in the media (T.V., radio, the press and journalism), the setters of moral trends, and those silent and powerful minorities in today's world who would seek to push us nearer to a godless and lawless society. We must heed the command to pray before it is too late. Prayer can be the deciding factor in the land in which we live. It can and will change people.

Not until the veil is drawn back over the record of history will we know what disasters and mistakes were prevented because people prayed, and what chaos and breakdown happened because we did not pray.

In the life of the local church

The Psalmist echoes what many Christians feel, long for, and are praying about the world and the church today: 'Restore us again, O God our Saviour. . . Will you not revive us again, that your people may rejoice in you?' (Ps. 85.4, 6). In parts of the world, especially the so-called Third World, in Africa, parts of South America, and in the East, the Church is making remarkable growth. In Britain, in Europe and in the more materially prosperous nations the Church is hardly holding its own. Although there is growth in the house churches, the Assemblies of God and the Black Pentecostal churches, there is a slow decline in the recorded membership of the mainline denominations. We long for revival and in revival, prayer is the decisive factor.

'There has never been a revival in a country or locality that did not begin with united prayer.' The words are

Dr Edwin Orr's, speaking at the City Temple in London in May 1983. For more than fifty years Dr Orr has studied the history and pattern of revivals around the world, and in history.

Dr Torrey makes the same point. 'Every true revival from that day to this has had its earthly origin in prayer. "The Great Awakening" under Jonathan Edwards in the eighteenth century began with his famous call to prayer, and he carried it forward by prayer. It has been recorded of Jonathan Edwards that he "so laboured in prayer that he wore the hard wooden boards into grooves where his knees pressed so often and so long".'[9]

The fastest growing church in the world today is almost certainly the Assemblies of God Church in Seoul, Korea, under the leadership of Dr Paul Yonggi Cho. He writes of revival: 'Evangelism is Good News. Revival is New Life. Evangelism is man working for God. Revival is God working in a sovereign way on man's behalf. Prayer is the key to revival. If revival is the sovereign work of the Holy Spirit, what causes the Holy Spirit to move upon the hearts of God's people bringing new power and greater boldness? The simple answer is prayer.'[10]

The thought of revival in our land may simply overwhelm us. Where does our small fellowship, or church, fit into this picture? Let me make some suggestions. Jeremiah 29.11 says: ' "I know the plans I have for you," declares the LORD, "plans to prosper you, and not to harm you, plans to give you a future and hope." ' Our task – if we are in a position of leadership in a local church or fellowship – is to seek the Lord in prayer and to pray down his plans and purposes. All too often we set up a committee and spend endless hours in unproductive discussion only to end with a split vote on what we think should be done! It would be much better to come together to pray down what the Lord would have us do. 'Goals are to be set upon our knees. They are not dreamed up, but prayed down.'[11] Once again, prayer is the deciding factor, for prayer changes people.

More than sixty years ago, Dr R. A. Torrey wrote words that are still true today: 'Prayer is the key that unlocks all the storehouses of God's infinite grace and power. . . Oh, any church can have a minister who is a man of power, a minister who is baptised and filled with the Holy Ghost if they are willing to pay the price, and the price is prayer, much prayer, and much real prayer, prayer in the Holy Ghost.'[12]

In our everyday lives

Every Christian, no matter how young in the faith or mature in God's service, has personal needs that must be met. We shall want our faith to grow and be strengthened, our lives to show more of the holiness of Jesus, to have our daily personal needs supplied, to be equipped and enabled to serve the Lord, and to be brought to wholeness of body, mind and spirit.

While there are different ways in which all these needs are met, there is one element common to all, and that is prayer. For example, the disciples, faced with the need to drive out an evil spirit from the epileptic son whose father came to them in great anxiety, had been defeated. (Matt. 17.19–21 and Mark 9.29). When the disciples asked Jesus why they had failed, He replied that this kind only comes out by prayer. Are there not times when we have been defeated in our Christian lives simply because we have not prayed? Yet, when we have truly prayed, we are able to rejoice in the victory that God gives.

On another occasion, Jesus promised His disciples that if they would seek first God's kingdom and His righteousness, then food, clothing and the secondary things of life would be given them as well (Matt. 6.33). I love that 'as well'. It is the Lord's bonus scheme for obedient disciples. As we look after the concerns and interests of our heavenly Father, so He will look after the concerns and interests of His earthly children.

Our needs are not only physical and outward, but

spiritual and inward. Here again, in the spiritual realm, we shall find things happening as prayer becomes the deciding factor. This truth dawned on me one afternoon when I sat down to read Paul's letters straight through – it was a rich feast with some lovely surprises. Not only was Paul revealed as a masterly letter writer, a much travelled missionary statesman, and a painstaking theologian (setting out the foundations of the faith so that others could build on them), in addition, two other characteristics also emerged. First, Paul had the evangelist's passionate heart that pleaded with men and women to come to faith in Christ. No trouble was too great and no pain too intense for him to suffer if only he might win men for Christ. Secondly, Paul was the caring pastor, watching over and faithfully praying for every young Christian, whether he had met them personally or not. He had never met the Christians at Colosse but he could write and tell them that he was praying daily for them that they might grow in holiness (Col. 1.9–10).

What a difference it would make in our lives and churches if we stopped criticising, judging, grumbling, complaining about and destroying one another, and instead began to pray that we and our fellow Christians would grow in holiness! Prayer can be the deciding factor and change people.

In our families

For most Christians, our homes are the places where our Christian faith is most tested. Parents long that their children should come to share their faith. Children are anxious that parents – especially as they get older and approach death – should know Christ personally. My experience as a parent and a minister is that we are willing to spend more time on our knees talking to God about our children, than we do talking to our children about God. But will prayer work? Is it fair?

The New Testament clearly teaches us that God wants everyone to have faith in Him:

(i) 'The Lord is not slow in keeping His promises, as some understand slowness. He is patient with you, not wanting anyone to perish, but everyone to come to repentance' (2 Pet. 3.9).

(ii) 'This is good, and pleases God our Saviour, who wants all men to be saved, and to come to a knowledge of the truth. For there is one God and one mediator between God and men, the man Christ Jesus' (1 Tim. 2.3–5).

Peter and Paul tell us that it is God's will for our loved ones to be saved. We are not taking an unfair advantage over them, even if they are hostile and opposed to the faith. Our prayers won't violate their personal freedom. We are praying that they will be set free from the power and clutches of the Evil One – Satan – and so be able to respond fully and freely of their own will to the claims of Jesus. Paul puts it like this to Timothy: 'Those who oppose him (the Lord's servant) he must gently instruct, in the hope that God will grant them repentance leading them to a knowledge of the truth, and that they will come to their senses and escape from the trap of the devil, who has taken them captive to do his will' (2 Tim. 2.25–26), and to the church at Corinth he says: 'The god of this age has blinded the minds of unbelievers, so that they cannot see the light of the gospel of the glory of Christ, who is the image of God. . . . For God, who said "Let light shine out of darkness," made his light shine in our hearts, to give us the light of the knowledge of the glory of God in the face of Christ' (2 Cor. 4.4, 6).

Satan wants to prevent children and parents understanding and responding to the Good News of Jesus, whereas God plans that we should see the light of the gospel. Prayer will be the deciding factor. Many families will find that to be true in the future, just as many families have found it to be true in the past.

Prayer is the deciding factor in our family life, our personal lives, in the welfare of society, in the life and growth of the church, in the constant spiritual battle, just as it was in the earthly life of the Lord Jesus Christ.

Just as it will always be in the spiritual battle and conflict between good and evil, between God and Satan.

You may have begun to glimpse the power and importance of prayer and now want to discover more. I hope that the rest of the book will help you. I want to show you the very strong foundations we have for prayer in the Father, the Son and the Holy Spirit. In them are found the three secrets of prayer which are available to all of us. I want you to understand how and why the world, the flesh and the devil try to hinder our prayers. We shall learn about some of the different aspects of prayer – confession, intercession, praise and listening to God.

The kaleidoscope of prayer may constantly change, but it should result in the glory of the Lord. To that end prayer will be the deciding factor.

Chapter One: Notes

1. S. D. Gordon, *Quiet Talks on Prayer* (Revell, New York, 9th Edition) p. 28.
2. From the hymn 'Prayer is the soul's sincere desire' by James Montgomery (1771–1854).
3. J. Oswald Sanders, *The Incomparable Christ* (Triangle/SPCK, 1984) pp. 136–7.
4. J. G. S. S. Thomson, *The Praying Christ* (Tyndale Press, 1961) p. 54.
5. S. D. Gordon, op. cit., p. 12.
6. Bob and Margaret Lunt's Prayer Letter from Juarez, Argentina, March 1985.
7. Andrew Murray, *With Christ in the School of Prayer* (Nisbet, 1902) p. 64.
8. R. A. Torrey, *The Power of Prayer* (Zondervan, 1977) pp. 51–5.
9. R. A. Torrey, op. cit., p. 187.
10. Paul Yonggi Cho, *More than Numbers* (Bridge, Plainfield, New Jersey, 1983) pp. 97 and 110.
11. Peter Cotterell, *Church Alive* (Inter-Varsity Press, Leicester, 1981) p. 93.
12. R. A. Torrey, op. cit., p. 40.

Two: Praying to the Father

I expect the first prayer that most people hear or say – and sometimes the only prayer they know – is what we call the Lord's Prayer. It begins: 'Our Father, who art in heaven. . .' and it ends: 'For thine is the kingdom, the power and glory'. Many people wonder to whom we should pray. Is it to Jesus, or the Holy Spirit or to God? There is a sense in which the Father, the Son and the Holy Spirit are all God so we may well find ourselves talking to the Spirit, or to the Lord Jesus, but prayer is really and primarily made to the Father. That was, after all, how Jesus taught His disciples to pray. (Matt. 6.9–11; Luke 11.2–4).

To us it is a familiar idea to pray to the Father. But for the disciples it was startlingly and staggeringly new. Previously, the disciples believed that prayer to God was limited to the liturgical prayers of the synagogue, expressed in such Psalms as Psalms 113–118 (known as the Hallel), and they were solely concerned with praise and the blessing of God as Creator, Provider and Covenant God. Even when the Early Church had been taught to call God 'Abba, Father', it regarded this as such a precious truth that the Lord's Prayer was not taught to believers until they had passed through the waters of baptism and had committed themselves to the fellowship of believers.

The meaning of 'Father'

The disciples, therefore, may have understood one of three things when Jesus referred to God as Father.

Firstly, they may have understood that God was their *Father-Creator*. There is much teaching in the Old Testament that would have emphasised this for them. For example:

> 'So God created man in His own image, in the image of God He created him; male and female He created them' (Gen. 1.27).

> 'Is this the way you repay the LORD, O foolish and unwise people? Is he not your Father, your Creator, who made you and formed you?' (Deut. 32.6).

> 'Have we not all one Father? Did not one God create us? Why do we profane the covenant of our fathers by breaking faith with one another?' (Mal. 2.10).

Secondly, they might have thought of God having a very special covenant relationship with Israel. Israel would be God's people, and God would be their God and Father:

> 'A son honours his father, and a servant his master. If I am a father, where is the honour due to me? If I am a master, where is the respect due to me?' says the LORD Almighty (Mal. 1.6).

Thirdly, the disciples might have done what we so often do, and think of God the Father in human terms. The child from a broken home, with a harsh father, thinks of God as harsh and unjust. The family where father is very frequently away on business may think of God as not available when needed. We are not to think of God the Father from our understanding of the human family. Rather, we are to learn what human fatherhood means by understanding what the New Testament tells us about the Fatherhood of God.

When Jesus teaches the disciples to address God as Father, He is not meaning that God is only Creator, neither is He implying that God has the faults of a human father. He is teaching His disciples that God is 'Abba, Father', and that is something excitingly new. (Mark 14.36; Rom. 8.15; Gal. 4.6).

'God – Abba, Father'

'Abba' was the word that Jesus used to describe His personal relationship with God, the Father. It is a homely and yet dignified Aramaic word that means 'Dearest Father'. We have to avoid two errors when thinking of God as 'Abba, Father'. On the one hand we must not be so familiar that we think of God as 'Daddy'. Nor must we be so overawed that God is remote and distant.

There is something else that is important about the word. Jesus didn't use the Hebrew language which was the holy languge of worship in the Temple or synagogue, but Aramaic, which was the usual language of everyday life. In *The Forgotten Father* Tom Smail writes: 'Jesus prays to Abba, a God too close to be appropriately addressed in the archaic language of long ago, because He is the living God today'.[1]

Jesus and the Father

What did 'Abba, Father' mean for Jesus? How did He understand God as the Father? It is important that we understand that, since what the word means for Jesus it can also mean for every Chrstian. We know that Jesus spoke of God as His Father in a special sense, but He also spoke of His Father as our Father. 'I am returning to my Father and your Father, to my God and your God' (John 20.17).

Firstly, Jesus *trusted* His Father simply and yet completely. We often forget that throughout His ministry the Lord exercised faith in His Father. When Jesus spoke words of healing, He expected people to get better; when he fed the five thousand, He believed there would be enough food to go round. He trusted in the Father. One remarkable instance of His faith was when

Jesus came to the tomb when His friend Lazarus had lain dead for four days. Jesus was about to raise him to life! He prayed to the Father: '. . . Father, I thank you that you have heard me. I knew that you always hear me. . .' (John 11.41–42). That was complete and unwavering trust in the Father.

Secondly, it meant *obedience* for Jesus. The nearer that Jesus came to the Cross, and the harder the way became – whether Jesus was praying in the Garden of Gethsemane, or hanging upon the Cross – He was still trusting and obeying and honouring His Father. 'Father, if you are willing, take this cup from me; yet not my will, but yours be done.' Or, 'Father, forgive them, for they do not know what they are doing.' Or, 'Father, into your hands I commit my spirit' (Luke 22.42; 23.34, 46).

At testing times we may find it hard to trust and obey God. Yet Jesus wants us to come to God as 'Abba, Father', the one we *can* tust when life is hard, when we face illness within the family, problems over finance, some big step of faith within the church, the call to change our work or whatever else it may be.

Don't get the impression that Jesus had a grim and unhappy relationship with His Father – some stern and all-powerful domineering Father – because it wasn't like that at all. It was a happy and joyful relationship. There were times when Jesus rejoiced in His spirit and His heart overflowed with praise to the Father (Luke 10.21). It was a close and loving relationship that Jesus had with His Heavenly Father (John 5.20; 10.30).

The Christian and God the Father

Jesus was teaching His disciples that God was not just their Creator. He was not just the Lord who had a special covenant relationship with His people. He was not like a human father with imperfections, but He was a loving, faithful Heavenly Father – 'Dearest Father', whom we could completely trust and utterly obey. Furthermore,

Jesus taught His disciples how God became their Father. Very simply they had to become members of His family.

Becoming a child of God

I sometimes ask people how they became a member of an earthly family. There are three ways! You can be born into a family, you can marry into a family, or you can be adopted into a family. The New Testament uses all three pictures to explain how we become members of God's family and God becomes our Father. In every case faith in Jesus is essential, and when I personally and actively trust Jesus as the Son of God who died upon the Cross for my sins and rose again to give me new life, then God gives me the right and privilege to become a member of His family. As John puts it: 'To all who received him, to those who believed in His name, he gave the right to become children of God – children born not of natural descent, nor of human decision or a husband's will, but born of God' (John 1.12–14).

So every committed Christian's spiritual birthright is to call God 'Abba, Father' (Romans 8.15–16). I wonder if you have begun to discover what that can mean for you in prayer?

Having God as our Father

It is St Paul, writing to the Christians at Ephesus, who sets out most clearly and simply what praying to God the Father means. He showed them that having God as Father meant at least four things – for them, and for us too.

(i) We can have *access to the Father*. 'For through him (Christ) we both have access to the Father by one Spirit' (Eph. 2.18). There is a marvellous picture behind that verse. Imagine that you are visiting Buckingham Palace and have the right to come into the Queen's presence. There will be the royal servant who ushers you in, and there will be the door you come through. The Holy Spirit is like the royal attendant who shows us into God's presence, and the door through which we enter is the door Christ opened for us when He died on the Cross. What a staggering privilege to come into the throne room of heaven and talk with the King of kings. None of us is worthy by himself, but Jesus has made it possible.

You will find that God's door is never closed. Our heavenly Father is open all hours. It will only be our sin and rebellion that closes the door. We can come to God the Father at any time and place, and find His peace and grace ever available to us.

(ii) Paul realises that we might fall into the trap of being overfamiliar with our heavenly Father, so he reminds us to *come with awe and reverence* to Him. 'I bow my knees before the Father, from whom the whole family in heaven and earth is named' (Eph. 3.14, RSV). The usual attitude for a praying Jew was to stand. Such is Paul's concern, burden and adoration that he falls on his knees before His Father. Jesus in a similar spirit fell on his face in Gethsemane (Matt. 26.39) because He was aware of the nearness of His Father, and yet conscious of His glory and greatness.

(iii) Paul writes about the *resources and authority of the Father*. 'I pray that out of His glorious riches He may strengthen you with power through His spirit in your inner being' (Eph. 3.16). A millionaire might give a five pound note from his riches, or he might give a ten thousand pound cheque out of, and according to, the size of his riches. God gives us the spiritual equivalent of a blank cheque to draw on the riches of His grace. Such is the extravagant power, spiritual authority and gracious liberality of our Heavenly Father.

David Watson once told the story of a farmer who gave away large sums of money and yet remained prosperous. People couldn't understand how this could happen, but the farmer said to them: 'It's like this. I keep shovelling into God's bin, and God keeps shovelling into my bin – but God has the bigger shovel.'[2]

(iv) Lastly, Paul expressed *adoration and praise* to His heavenly Father. That note was often found in his letters – even those that were written under difficult prison conditions (Eph. 3.1, 5.20). Paul knew that praise and adoration make a radical difference when praying to the Father.

Let me try and sum up what praying to the Father meant for both Paul and Jesus. Jesus refers to our daily bread, so presumably we are to pray to our Father daily, and not just when we feel like it, or happen to have some spare time. He teaches us about the Kingdom of God, on the one hand, and the slightest sin on the other – so that nothing is too big or too small to bring to our Father in prayer. Jesus teaches us that while we come as children to our Father, we also come as sinners to the Saviour, and as subjects to the King. We are never to use prayer as a way of twisting God's arm to get our own way and will done. It is not the short cut to get a difficult job done, nor a quick way to get ourselves out of a mess. Above everything else, when we pray to our Father in heaven we are expressing our desire for His glory and our dependence on His grace.

Two sides to the relationship

So far we have concentrated upon what this relationship means for us as children of God. Jesus also taught His disciples what the relationship meant from God's side. It is not a one-sided relationship in which we extract a meagre response from a reluctant God. God, our Father, is more willing and eager to give than ever we are to ask and receive.

In the Sermon on the Mount Jesus pictures our heavenly Father as always more ready to give than His children are to ask. God longs to respond to our prayers, and He knows what we need even before we ask. 'Pray to your Father, who is unseen. Then your Father, who sees what is done in secret, will reward you. . . Your Father knows what you need before you ask Him' (Matt. 6.6, 8).

It is not a matter of 'catching God at the right moment' or 'when He is in the mood to listen'. He doesn't change, and He doesn't short-change us. He is the God and Father who longs to go on giving. A literal translation of Luke 11.13 would read: 'Your heavenly Father goes on being willing to go on giving the Holy Spirit to those who go on asking Him.'

Dr Andrew Murray echoes these points:–

> 'Do not think of how little you have to bring to God, but of how much He wants to give you. . . . He who lets God be Father always and in everything will experience most gloriously that a life in God's infinite Fatherliness and continual answers to prayer are inseparable. . . . The chief lesson in the school of prayer is to be able to say 'Abba' Father. He that can say this, has the key to all prayer.'[3]

Let me stress this wonderful truth in another way. Often when Jesus spoke about God the Father He would describe Him in some special way. For example, the Father always gives good gifts (Matt. 7.11); He is the Lord of heaven and earth (Matt. 11.25–27); He is merciful (Luke 6.36); He is holy (Luke 11.2); He is righteous (John 17.25); He is perfect (Matt. 5.48); the Father is compassionate (2 Cor. 1.3); He is the glorious Father (Eph. 1.17), who is utterly fair and without favourites or bias in the family (1 Pet. 1.17).

Faced with this overwhelming evidence about God, we must surely agree with Professor Finlayson's comments about God the Father: 'The New Testament brings out the tender aspects of God's character, His love, His watchful care, His bounty and His faithfulness.'[4]

When Jesus began to teach His disciples to pray to

God as 'Our Father, who art in heaven', He didn't want them to think of God as Creator, or as a Covenant God only, but as one who longed to have a rich and genuine and personal relationship with His children, whoever they happened to be, through faith in Jesus.

It is this experience that explains Jesus' words in John 16.23, 'In that day you will no longer ask me anything. I tell you the truth, my Father will give you whatever you ask in my name.' No longer would the disciples have to rely upon Jesus 'doing their praying for them', they would be able to speak directly to the Father themselves. There are some Christians who still need to learn that lesson. They are the Christians who don't feel worthy, who believe that someone else will do a better job than they in praying to the Father. They may be lazy Christians, or untaught Christians, but all Christians have the right to come to the Father themselves.

If this is not a real experience for you there may be something wrong between your heavenly Father and yourself! It won't be from the Father's side, but it may be on your side. Jesus was quite plain in teaching us about the privileges and the responsibilities of having God as our Father.

Our responsibility when praying to the Father

We can sum up our responsibility in three ways.

(i) If we want to enjoy our relationship with our Heavenly Father, then we must be willing to *forgive others* – whether they are Christians or not. This condition of prayer is stressed probably more than any other in the whole of the New Testament. Jesus understood that the 'bottom line' as to whether we really wanted God to forgive us, and understood our need to be forgiven, was whether we were willing to forgive others. Jesus goes so far as to say that if we have not forgiven someone, if we are holding a grudge, hanging on to a spirit of resentment, shutting our hearts against anyone – whoever it is – then we shall not know the reality of forgiveness and peace and access with the Father.

> 'And when you stand praying, if you hold anything against anyone, forgive him, so that your Father in heaven may forgive you your sins. But if you do not forgive, neither will your Father who is in heaven forgive your sins' (Mark 11.25–26).

> 'Be kind and compassionate to one another, forgiving each other, just as in Christ God forgave you' (Eph. 4.32).

Our English word 'forgive' hides the fact that the original Greek of the New Testament uses two different words for forgiving. One word meant 'to release from a debt, or to remove a burden, or to stop holding a grudge or a complaint against another person'. A second word (used here in Eph. 4.32) meant 'to unconditionally bestow a favour, or to give a blessing to another'. God wants us to see that when He asks us to forgive, we not only remove any barriers to the fellowship, but we positively long for the blessing of our brother or sister.

(ii) If we want to enjoy our relationship with the Father, we shall need to *obey Him*. 'Not everyone who says to me, "Lord, Lord," will enter the kingdom of heaven, but only he who does the will of my Father who is in heaven' (Matt. 7.21); or 'If anyone loves me, he will obey my teaching. My Father will love him, and we will come to him and make our home with him' (John 14.23).

(iii) If we want to enjoy our relationship with the Father, we must *trust Him*. This point is well illustrated by TEAR Fund Director, George Hoffman. Reviewing the first fifteen years of the Fund's existence, he writes: 'Within many Christian communities throughout the developing world, I have discerned what seems to be a correlation between their subsistence economy and a heightened spiritual awareness. They say: "In your country you have God and things. Here we just have God." Prayer among some of the poorest Christians I have met is not looked upon as a programmed devotional or an S.O.S. help-line. It is a way of life.'[5]

Such people may be poor in material possessions, but they are wealthy in spiritual experience because they have learned to trust their heavenly Father.

Prayer for the believer begins to make sense when we realise that we don't have to try harder, pray longer, or believe more intensely. We discover from the pages of the Bible, and the teaching of Jesus, that we can have a living, loving, permanent and personal relationship with God as Abba, Father. 'God as Father is the key to the problem of prayer.'[6]

No longer is He the impersonal, austere Creator who is unaware of our needs and nature. 'Abba, Father' is the active, loving, compassionate, holy and almighty heavenly Father, who, while asking His children to be forgiving, obedient and trusting, longs to give them the very best that is possible.

So Jesus, when He began to teach His disciples to pray, said 'This is how you are to pray' . . . 'Our Father.'

Chapter Two: Notes

1. Tom Smail, *The Forgotten Father* (Hodder and Stoughton, 1980) p. 161.
2. David Watson, *Renewal* (January 1985), p. 127.
3. Andrew Murray, *With Christ in the School of Prayer* (Nisbet, 1902) pp. 19, 43–4.
4. R. A. Finlayson, 'God the Father', *The New Bible Dictionary* (Inter-Varsity Fellowship, 1962).
5. TEAR Fund Annual Report 1984.
6. Samuel Chadwick, *The Path of Prayer* (Hodder and Stoughton, 1931) p. 66.

Three: Praying in the Name of Jesus

Jesus taught His disciples to pray to the Father, and to pray in His name. He taught them that there would come a time when they would no longer have to address their requests to Him but they would be able to pray for themselves in His name.

> 'In that day you will no longer ask me anything. I tell you the truth, my Father will give you whatever you ask in my name. Until now you have not asked for anything in my name. Ask and you will receive, and your joy will be complete' (John 16.23–24).

In those few words Jesus sums up two of the three keys of prayer. Prayer must be to the Father and in the name of the Lord Jesus. (We shall discover in the next chapter that prayer must also be through the Holy Spirit.) The Father provides us with the relationship that makes prayer possible, the Son gives us the resources that makes prayer powerful, and the Holy Spirit makes prayer a personal reality for us.

May we never forget that in the three persons of the Trinity – Father, Son and Holy Spirit – we have been given the firmest foundations on which to build our prayer lives, and they matter.

Foundations matter especially in volcanic areas of the world, where the shaking and tremors of an earthquake can rock whole cities and do untold damage. One such volcanic area is to be found around Arequipa, the second largest city of Peru in South America, where a group of missionaries, drawn from America, Britain, and Peru, were beginning to build their new church in order to have room to accommodate the congregation. It was necessary to dig down as deeply as they could go to lay the foundations. In the process they had to remove rocks and boulders, but eventually came to a layer of rock through which they couldn't go, and on this they laid the foundations. It was hard work to dig down and get to those foundations, but on these foundations they have built not only the church, but living accommodation, and a book room, so that they can reach up to the Lord in prayer, and out to the city in evangelism and service.

It may be hard work to dig our foundations for prayer, but if we do so, we will be able to reach up to the Lord in fellowship, and out to others in love and service.

The phrase 'in the name of Jesus' is the second key to effective praying.

In the name of Jesus

We are to pray 'in the name of Jesus' just as we are to do everything in His name – for example, we are to baptise, call upon, anoint with oil, ask, command, suffer reproach for, rejoice, preach, give thanks, be justified, do all, forgive, believe, confess, cast out . . . all in the name of Jesus. It is His name, His authority and His power by which we act. Jesus could not have made it clearer. As the Lord came to the close of His earthly ministry He took the disciples aside to teach them the things that really mattered about following Him, and building His church. He taught them (John chapters 13–16) about humble service, about the gift and ministry of the Holy Spirit, about loving one another, about the attitude that the world would have towards them, about their continuing, abiding relationship with Him, and about prayer. And when Jesus taught them about prayer it was always to be in His name.

'I tell you the truth, anyone who has faith in me will

do what I have been doing. He will do even greater things than these, because I am going to the Father. And I will do whatever you ask *in my name*, so that the Son may bring glory to the Father. You may ask me for anything *in my name*, and I will do it' (John 14.12–14).

'In that day you will no longer ask me anything. I tell you the truth, my Father will give you whatever you ask *in my name*. Until now you have not asked for anything *in my name*. Ask and you will receive, and your joy will be complete' (John 16.23–24).

The same emphasis is found in many of the church's hymns and spiritual songs: 'At the Name of Jesus', 'Jesus, name above all Names', 'Jesus, the Name high over all'.

The meaning of 'The name'

The name isn't just the title on the outside, it is the substance and contents in reality. 'The name' is used often in the New Testament, but never explained. The early Christians must have grasped quickly what Jesus meant. The character, the person, the authority, the rule, the power, the total expression of who Jesus is and what He has done. I fear that is not always true for later generations of Christians. If I were to give my personal church safe keys to a member of the congregation, and to tell him to use them in my name whenever he needed to, I would be putting at his disposal (but taking the responsibility for) and trusting him with all and anything in the safe – the records and registers, silver and plate, money and cheques that might happen to be there. Jesus has likewise given us the key 'in His name'.

'The name of Jesus' implies four things:

(i) *The name = the merits of Jesus' work* When Jesus told the story of the religious leader and the tax collector

(Luke 18.9–14), he pictured the Pharisee telling God all about the good things he had done for God. 'I thank you that I am not like all other men – robbers, evildoers, adulterers – or even like this tax collector. I fast twice a week and give a tenth of all I get' (verses 11–12). By contrast, the tax collector couldn't look God in the face. He stood at a distance, and beat upon his breast and said, 'God, have mercy on me, a sinner' (verse 13). The Pharisee told God how good he was, the tax collector how bad he was. The first told God what he had done for Him. The second asked God to do something for him. The first came in his own name, the second came only in the name of God. We are able to draw near to God solely in the name of Jesus, we have no right to come in our own name, but we have every right to come in the name of the Lord Jesus if He is our Saviour.

I do not naturally have a right to come into God's presence. He is utterly holy and good and pure, and I am selfish and rebellious and a sinner. But because Jesus died upon the Cross to deal with my sin and rebellion and disobedience, and now invites me, by faith, to draw near to God, I am able to do so in the name of Jesus, and the Holy Spirit brings me into the presence of the King of kings. That is the right and privilege of every Christian.

The writer to the Hebrews sums it up like this: 'Therefore, brothers, since we have confidence to enter the Most Holy Place by the blood of Jesus, by a new and living way opened for us through the curtain, that is, his body, and since we have a great priest over the house of God, let us draw near to God with a sincere heart in full assurance of faith, having our hearts sprinkled to cleanse us from a guilty conscience and having our bodies washed with pure water. 'Let us hold unswervingly to the hope we profess, for he who promised is faithful' (Heb. 10.19–23).

It is no use telling God how long we have been a Christian, what we have done for Him, and why He should answer our prayers and coming in our own name before Him. Whoever we are we come to God solely in the name of Jesus. That name is our passport to heaven and it will never be out of date or invalid because Jesus himself is seated at God's right hand as we come to the Father in His name.

(ii) *The name = The greatness of Jesus' riches* Christians have no reason to be spiritually poor, since we have at our disposal all the riches of Christ. Consider what Paul wrote about the riches of Christ to the Church at Ephesus.

> In him (Christ) we have redemption through His blood, the forgiveness of sins, in accordance with the *riches of God's grace* that He lavished on us with all wisdom and understanding.
>
> 'I pray . . . that you may know . . . the *riches of His glorious inheritance* in the saints. . .'
>
> 'God, who is *rich in mercy*, made us alive with Christ . . . (to) show the incomparable *riches of His grace*, expressed in His kindness to us in Christ Jesus.'
>
> 'This grace was given me: to preach . . . *the unsearchable riches of Christ* . . . I pray that out of *His glorious riches* He may strengthen you' (Eph. 1.7, 18; 2.4, 7; 3.8, 16).

Paul was always careful and precise in the words he used, and quite deliberately he speaks of God's grace to us in Christ as His riches lavished on us, incomparable, unsearchable and glorious, and they are intended for *us* and available in Christ. They are the riches of being set free from sin, and knowing the burden of sin being lifted off and taken away – that deals with the past. The riches of being strengthened inwardly by His Spirit deals with the present, and the incomparable riches of our inheritance is a promise for the future. In just a few phrases

Paul displays the extravagant wealth available to Christians who will draw upon the unlimited resources of God's grace in and through Christ.

When we come to God in faith and in the name of Jesus we call humbly upon all the means, resources, wealth and riches that God has for us in Christ. Annie Flint's poem catches the same truth about the generous grace of God for us.

He giveth more grace when the burdens grow
  greater,
He sendeth more strength when the labours
  increase;
To added affliction He addeth His mercy.
To multiplied trials, His multiplied peace.

When we have exhausted our store of endurance,
When our strength has failed ere the day is half
  done,
When we reach the end of our hoarded resources,
Our Father's full giving is only begun.

His love has no limit, His grace has no measure,
His power no boundary known unto men;
For out of His infinite riches in Jesus
He giveth and giveth and giveth again.[1]

If we go to God in prayer in our name, we only go with our spiritual poverty and emptiness, but if we go 'in the name of Jesus' we are able to draw from our Lord inexhaustible supplies of grace. If we are not able to go to God *with* what He commands, then we come to God *for* what He commands. Such are His riches.

(iii) *The motive and will of Jesus* Praying in the name of Jesus means that we shall pray with the same purpose, motive and will that Jesus prayed. Just as Jesus prayed according to the will of His Father, so we shall pray according to the will of the Son.

'This is the assurance we have in approaching God:

that if we ask anything according to His will, He hears us. And if we know that He hears us – whatever we ask, we know that we have what we asked of Him' (1 John 5.14–15).

For most, if not all, Christians there is the problem of not being sure what God's will is, and because we don't know, we don't pray with assurance.

God wants us to pray along the lines of His will, and so He has given us three very important guidelines.

Firstly, we have the word of God, the Bible. It is the revelation of what God wants, and as we pray in line with the teaching of the Bible in general, and specific promises in particular, we can be sure that we are praying according to His will.

For example, can we pray with confidence for the conversion of men and women? The Bible's reply is very clearly 'Yes', because God longs that all should be saved and come to the knowledge of the truth (1 Tim. 2.4). The Bible, therefore, not only directs our praying, but also promotes faith when we pray. 'Faith comes from what is heard, and what is heard comes by the preaching of Christ' (Rom. 10.17, RSV).

Secondly, we have the Spirit of God to direct our prayers. (We shall look at this in detail in another chapter). We can claim the promise that 'the Spirit helps us in our weakness. We do not know what we ought to pray, but the Spirit himself intercedes for us with groans that words cannot express. And he who searches our hearts knows the mind of the Spirit, because the Spirit intercedes for the saints in accordance with God's will' (Rom. 8.26–27).

Thirdly, we are to allow the peace of Christ to rule in our hearts (Col. 3.15). In the same way that an umpire in a tennis match will rule whether the ball landed in or out of the court, so God's peace within our hearts can tell us whether something is in harmony with God's will, or in conflict with it.

Let me give you an example. We know that God is a just God, and that the gospel is about justice and love.

Therefore if our prayers are concerned with an issue of justice – fair business, equality between black and white, protection for the weak, support for the family, or purity in our national life – just to mention a few areas for prayerful concern – we know that these issues are according to the will of the Lord for 'Righteousness and justice are the foundation of your throne; love and faithfulness go before you' (Ps. 89.14).

(iv) *The manner in which Jesus prayed* The last part of understanding what praying 'in the name of Jesus' means highlights the way or the manner in which Jesus prayed. Jesus came to His Father in simple trust and in humble obedience. He prayed specifically and regularly. The more we can reflect the prayer life of the Master, the more we shall find ourselves praying as He prayed, and in His name.

The Conditions

If Jesus has given us His staggering promises, on the one hand, He has also made quite clear the simple conditions we are to fulfil in order to receive them. *We are to love and obey Him.*

'You may ask me for anything in my name, and I will do it. If you love me, you will obey what I command' and 'Dear friends, if our hearts do not condemn us, we have confidence before God and receive from Him anything we ask, because we obey His commands, and do what pleases Him, and this is His command: to believe in the name of His Son, Jesus Christ, and to love one another as He commanded us' (John 14.14–15, 1 John 3.21–23).

'Again, I tell you that if two of you on earth agree about anything you ask for, it will be done for you by my Father in heaven. For where two or three come together in my name, there am I with them' (Matt. 18.19–20).

The staggering promises given by Jesus can lead to

exciting possibilities when two or three people, loving and obeying the Lord meet to pray. The two or three may be friends in a tower block, or street, they may be colleagues in an office or factory, young people at school or college, a husband and wife. Such small groups of believers meeting all round the world can be the most powerful spiritual force for good and for God that is possible. It is an exciting and realistic vision.

Personal private prayer has the advantage that prayer can be individual, immediate, intimate and intense in a way that is not always possible in a small group or prayer cell. But two or three believers, gathered in the name of Jesus, will stimulate each other's faith and vision. It will encourage us when we falter and find the going tough. The fellowship in Christ's name will enrich our spirit, and make the presence of the living Lord such that we shall want to reach out and touch Him as He stands in our midst by His Spirit.

A testimony that prayer works

Let me share with you a testimony.

John lay in a hospital bed having suffered a brain haemorrhage at the start of a third term of missionary service far from home. Suddenly the future of his missionary service, the welfare of his wife and two small children, and even his life was in doubt. People, literally around the world – individually and in groups – turned to the Lord for John, 'in Jesus' name'. John was brought home. The best surgeons investigated and took repeated tests. The anticipated operation was not needed, and John is now back in a demanding job in this country. Writing of that time, in a letter to me, he said:

> I found it relatively easy to perform the daily devotional routine, but during the time of the haemorrhage and since we have found a much deeper reality in prayer which is not necessarily based on set times and positions (as important as they are). Prayer has

become far more of a conscious walk with the Lord each day, knowing His presence in each thought and fear and even breath.

The promises of God have taken on a far more vital and personal nature. It is so easy to leave these promises as sterile doctrine. Having been forced to 'taste and see' just how real those promises of peace and rest are, I hope that we have learned how to claim God's promises for each day.

Prayer has also given us an insight into how real the worldwide universal Church really is. To have received messages literally from all over the world, and to know that the prayers offered by those friends have been answered in the most wonderful way just makes me realise what an incredible body we belong to.[2]

John might also have added – what an incredible privilege we have to pray 'in the name of Jesus'.

The power of the name

Praying 'in the name of Jesus' is the key we have been given to unlock the secrets and power of prayer. We have seen that it has four parts: we come to the Lord in the name of Jesus relying upon the merits of His saving work on the Cross; we come to the Lord knowing that the infinite wealth of Jesus is available to answer our prayers; we pray in the name of Jesus when our prayers are according to the will of Jesus; and we pray 'in His name' as we fashion our attitude to the Father to reflect the attitude that Jesus had. (Incidentally, we are never told in the Bible to pray 'for Jesus' sake' – though many Christians use that phrase. Our prayers will be for Jesus' and the Father's glory, yet they will be for our sake or the sake of others, and 'in His name'.)

Samuel Chadwick has summed it up like this: 'The most incredible things are promised in prayer. To pray in the name of Christ is to pray as one who is at one with Christ, whose mind is the mind of Christ, whose desires are the desires of Christ, and whose purpose is one with that of Christ.'[3]

Prayer ceases to be a routine duty, and becomes an exciting prospect. We stop seeing prayer as something that might work from time to time, and begin to see it as a powerful and fruitful ministry for the believer. That lifts the prayer meeting to the highest level of importance and priority for the church. It means that instead of being a poorly attended church meeting, the prayer meeting should become the best attended. Instead of it being the last meeting some people will come to, it should become the first. Our times of prayer will take on a whole new meaning and reality.

As Andrew Murray puts it: 'A prayer meeting without recognised answers to prayer ought to be an anomaly. . . . Jesus has, by His promise, consecrated every assembly in His Name to be a Gate of Heaven where His presence is to be felt and His Power experienced in the Father fulfilling their desires.'[4]

Sadly, few of us have found this to be consistently so, but let us exalt the name of Jesus so that we might once more receive what Jesus has promised us. 'Ask and it will be given to you; seek and you will find; knock and the door will be opened to you. For everyone who asks receives; he who seeks finds; and to him who knocks, the door will be opened' (Matt. 7.7–8).

Chapter Three: Notes

1. Annie Johnson Flint, *But God* (Zondervan, 21st edition, 1974).
2. Rev. John Sutton, Youth Secretary of the South American Missionary Society in a personal letter, September 1984.
3. Samuel Chadwick, *The Path of Prayer* (Hodder & Stoughton, 1931) pp. 49 and 52.
4. Andrew Murray, *With Christ in the School of Prayer* (Nisbet, 1902) pp. 113 and 116.

Four: Praying in the Spirit

Bill, the headmaster of a local junior school and a member of our congregation, invited me to look around the school. It was during the Christmas holidays, and everywhere was locked. As we arrived at the gate, he dragged out from his overcoat pocket the most amazing bunch of keys I have ever seen. There must have been twenty or thirty keys, large and small, to fit every conceivable door, store room, boiler house or gate.

Some Christians feel that they have to possess a similar bunch of spiritual keys if they would unlock all the doors and store houses into the riches of prayer. I'm grateful that our heavenly Father has given us just three keys. The first is finding a living relationship with God as our heavenly Father, and ourselves as His children, so that prayer is talking with God. The second we have just considered – praying in the name of Jesus. The last key is to 'pray in the Spirit'.

Let me say at once that some Christians are too vague, and other Christians too narrow, about this phrase and relate it just to 'praying in tongues'. But the New Testament is very specific about it.

The meaning of 'in the Spirit'

The Christian life is lived either 'in the Spirit' or 'in the flesh' – and we shall deal fully with 'the flesh' in chapter six.

> 'For those who live according to the flesh set their minds on the things of the flesh, but those who live

according to the Spirit set their minds on the things of the Spirit. To set the mind on the flesh is death, but to set the mind on the Spirit is life and peace. For the mind that is set on the flesh is hostile to God; it does not submit to God's law, indeed it cannot; and those who are in the flesh cannot please God' (Rom. 8.5–8, RSV).

'But I, brethren, could not address you as spiritual men, but as men of the flesh, ... For while there is jealousy and strife among you, are you not the flesh, and behaving like ordinary men?' (1 Cor. 3.1, 3, RSV).

'But I say, walk by the Spirit, and do not gratify the desires of the flesh. For the desires of the flesh are against the Spirit, and the desires of the Spirit are against the flesh; for these are opposed to each other, to prevent you from doing what you would' (Gal. 5.16–17, RSV).

Paul then goes on (in Gal. 5.19f) to list what are known as the works of the flesh, on the one hand, and the fruit of the Spirit – love, joy, peace, patience, kindness, etc. – on the other.

Every Christian allows either the Holy Spirit or the flesh (self-life) to be in control. That is true wherever we are and whatever we are doing – working, playing, travelling, worshipping or praying.

If we are going to know the reality of praying in the Spirit, we must be living and walking in the Holy Spirit. As Andrew Murray says: 'It is living in the Name of Christ that is the secret of praying in the Name of Christ. Living in the Spirit that fits us for praying in the Spirit.'[1]

What is true for the Christian life generally, is specifically true for praying. Indeed, we are commanded to 'pray in the Spirit', and as R. A. Torrey has written 'The whole secret of prayer is found in those words "in the Spirit".'[2]

Paul says:

'In the same way, the Spirit helps us in our weakness. We do not know what we ought to pray, but the Spirit himself intercedes for us with groans that words cannot express. And he who searches our hearts knows the mind of the Spirit, because the Spirit intercedes for the saints in accordance with God's will' (Rom. 8.26–27).

'And pray in the Spirit on all occasions with all kinds of prayers and requests. With this in mind, be alert and always keep on praying for all the saints' (Eph. 6.18).

Jude tells us:

'But you, dear friends, build yourselves up in your most holy faith and pray in the Holy Spirit. Keep yourselves in God's love as you wait for the mercy of our Lord Jesus Christ to bring you to eternal life' (Jude 20–21).

The need to pray in the Spirit

We are to 'pray in the Spirit' for two reasons. Firstly, prayer expresses our relationship with God, and God is a Spirit. If God were physical, then we would be able to relate on the physical level, but God is a Spirit. That is why Jesus said (John 4) that those who worship aright must worship in Spirit and in truth. The woman, who had come to the well to draw water, was concerned which was the right place to worship God—was it 'this mountain' or 'in Jerusalem'—but Jesus tells her that the true worshippers will worship in Spirit and in truth. 'God is spirit, and his worshippers must worship in spirit and in truth' (John 4.24). It is not the outward details of worship that are essential, but the inward devotion of the human heart. That is why Jesus himself prayed in the Spirit (Luke 10.21).

The second reason concerns our weakness. We need

the work and help of the Spirit to overcome our weaknesses in prayer. We may not know exactly what to pray for, and so we need the help of the Spirit. We may not find it easy to believe for what we are praying; we may not find it easy to continue in prayer until we receive the answer, we may be going through a period of depression, and so in every case we need the ministry of the Spirit.

We would all confess we are weak, when we come to pray, if we are honest with God and ourselves. That should not hinder our praying – rather it should encourage us to pray.

The ministry of the Spirit

The Bible is full of pictures which help us to 'see' what God is saying. One such picture is that of the ambassador or representative of another country. We send our ambassador, embassy staff, representative or trade delegations to other nations throughout the world to speak and work on behalf of our nation. Those nations, in their turn, send their ambassadors and embassy staff to this country to speak for them. Sometimes the rules of diplomacy are broken, relationships are broken off, and the representatives are asked to leave and go home. For every country two ambassadors are involved – their ambassador in our country and our ambassador in their country. And so it is with God. We are told that the Lord Jesus is our ambassador with God at the Court of heaven and that the Holy Spirit is God's representative to the Christian here on earth.

'If any one does sin, we have an *advocate* with the Father, Jesus Christ the righteous' (1 John 2.1, RSV).

'I will pray the Father, and He will give you another *Counsellor*, to be with you for ever, even the Spirit of truth, whom the world cannot receive, because it neither sees Him nor knows Him; you know Him, for He dwells with you, and will be in you' (John 14.16–17).

The Greek word for both the advocate and the counsellor is 'Paraclete', the helper or representative. The Holy Spirit is the person called in to help us in our weakness.

In my Christian ministry, I am sometimes called in to help others with a particular problem. Indeed as I was writing these words, the telephone went with just such a request. A family will report a strange coldness in the house, which has nothing to do with the physical temperature of the house. It may be that a child is unable to sleep undisturbed in a certain bedroom, or that there are strange movements of furniture, all of which witness to some strange spiritual presence. Most of us feel unqualified to minister alone, and so we ask the help of another Christian worker. I am only able to help others because earlier in my experience and weakness I asked another Christian to help and minister to me.

That is a little of what the Holy Spirit wants to do for us. In our weakness He makes us strong. Thus, prayer is never something that we do on our own. We have the promise of the Holy Spirit to help us.

How the Holy Spirit helps our praying

How, in practice, does the Holy Spirit help me pray?

(i) The Holy Spirit will use the Scriptures, the Word of God. Paul tells us to 'take the Sword of the Spirit, which is the word of God' (Eph. 6.17). There are two words that describe the Scriptures. One is 'Logos' which refers to the complete revelation of God's will for us. It is the Bible. The other is 'Rhema' which means a particular word of God, a verse or a passage of Scripture, that is God's precise instruction or promise for a given situation. In addition, we may well receive a word of prophecy or a word of wisdom or knowledge personally or through the fellowship.

Let me give you two illustrations. On one occasion six of us were praying for a young child in the church who was very seriously ill, and we did not know how to pray. As we were waiting in the silence I found the words 'Put her into my hands' coming across my mind, in the same way as I had seen the teleprinter type out the football results on the TV. I shared these words with the rest of the group, and one of the other men, my churchwarden, said he had been given exactly the same words. We knew how to pray through a word from the Holy Spirit. We entrusted the child into the hands of the Lord, and shortly afterwards she died in a London hospital.

The second occasion happened during our church prayer meeting. I forget what we were praying about, but suddenly my elder daughter came in to tell us that our nephew had suffered a car crash and was in intensive care with broken ribs and very severe internal damage. We were later to discover the amazing providence of the Lord in each detail of the subsequent events, but as we turned to pray for David I found those words in John 11 came to me; 'This illness is not unto death, but for the glory of God.' God's Spirit had come with that very personal and relevant word. Later that night I drove the forty miles to Guildford and shared that message with David's parents as we anxiously waited for news from the operating theatre. They were words that kept us trusting as we prayed through each crisis over the next ten days. I still recall, with a lump in my throat, the thrill on Christmas Day – just eight weeks later – of seeing David walking into our house looking as if nothing had happened. It was for the glory of God.

The Spirit and the word of God go hand in hand. We are not to sress the ministry of the Holy Spirit apart from the word of God, for that can lead to excess and extremism; nor are we to major on the Scripture without the Spirit, for that will lead to dullness and barrenness. I rejoice in a faith made alive both through the ministry of the word of God and the Spirit of God.

(ii) The Holy Spirit will help us to pray with perseverance. When Paul instructed the Ephesian Christians to pray in the Spirit, it was to be at all times, and with all prayer and supplication, with all perseverance for all the saints (Eph. 6.18). The word 'all' comes four times, and we find this a difficult instruction to carry out. We can pray for some time, for some people (we may also find it easier to pray for some people than others); but when the Holy Spirit is prompting and directing the praying He enables us to persevere.

When we pray for those near and dear to us, our emotions will be involved, but this doesn't mean that we are not praying in the Spirit. The early Church felt very emotional about Peter shut up in prison facing certain death the following morning and they prayed (Acts 12.5). They kept at it, inspired both by their human spirit and by the Holy Spirit. How do we keep at it when those emotions are absent, and when the circumstances are not so pressing? The Holy Spirit helps us in our weakness. Of coure, He expects our co-operation. We have got to be willing to pray – even if we do not feel like it. He transforms our weakness.

(iii) The Holy Spirit will help us to pray with confident assurance. I love that incident in Acts 4.23–31 when Peter and John had been released back to their friends. They had been imprisoned for healing, in the name of Jesus, the lame beggar who had lain at the Beautiful Gate of the Temple and then preaching about Jesus to the crowd who had quickly gathered together as a result. Undeterred, the apostles came back to their friends, praised God that He was sovereign and in control, prayed that they might know the filling of and the boldness of the Spirit to go out to witness, and for the Lord to heal. They were praying in the Spirit. The endowment of the Spirit was both the cause and the consequence of their effectual praying. They prayed because they were filled, and they were filled because they prayed. It was a victorious, rather than a vicious circle.

The conditions required

The Holy Spirit is always ready to help us pray, but there are conditions we need to fulfil:

(i) The Holy Spirit will help us pray if we are willing to confess known sin. Imagine two people on their way to worship. They have a disagreement and come into the church having to pretend that all is well. If they don't get themselves right with God and right with each other, it is not surprising that they come out of church saying they didn't get anything out of the worship and the address! After all, if you are harbouring a grudge against the preacher, how can you expect to appreciate the sermon. (Conversely, believing prayer for one's Vicar, minister or church leaders can bring blessing all round!) The Spirit who helps us in our weakness is a Holy Spirit, and He demands holiness in our lives if we would know His power and direction.

(ii) The Holy Spirit will help us in prayer when we take time for Him to lead us. God is never in a hurry. Yet, how often do we Christians go through the motions of praying to ease our conscience? We wave a list of names in God's direction and kid ourselves that we are 'praying in the Spirit'. We need to be very practical and realistic. We have to make time for prayer. We make time for everything else that we consider important, so why not prayer?

A recent survey has revealed that the average British man or woman watches more than twenty-one hours of television every week – an average of three hours every day. I expect that the average Christian watches much less, but I also suspect that the average Christian spends more time before his

TV or video than he does before God and the Throne of Grace!

In *The Cross and the Switchblade*, David Wilkerson of Teen Challenge tells of the radical difference in his life and ministry, and consequently in the lives and ministries of others, when he switched off the TV and switched onto the Lord and began praying in the Spirit. It takes time and commitment, but God will mightily bless.

What it means in practice

Praying in the Spirit may be expressed in various ways. Dr Jim Packer has written:

> Prayer in the Spirit is prayer from the heart, springing from awareness of God, of self, of others, of needs and of Christ. Whether it comes forth verbalised, as with the prayers and praises recorded in Scripture, or unverbalised, as when the contemplative gazes God-ward in love or when the charismatic slips into glossal-aiia, is immaterial. He whose heart seeks God through Christ prays in the Spirit.[3]

We might well add to this helpful definition that praying in the Spirit will include the unexpected, sudden burden and 'nudging' from God for some person or situation. Christians in two or three places in the British Isles were prompted to pray for Bishop Hassan Dehqani-Tafti, when he was Bishop of Iran. They did not know why, but were later to find out that at that precise moment he and his wife were being attacked by gunmen in their home in Teheran, and the Bishop had escaped with his life. You may 'out of the blue' be burdened to pray for a friend, or a member of the family or a missionary far away. At the time you don't know why, but you may well discover God's leading by his Spirit in circumstances where your knowledge or wisdom was inadequate.

Such praying in the Spirit does not contradict being quite practical and specific in our prayers. For example, the fact that we are seeking to pray in the Spirit 'at all times' does not lessen the need for specific times of prayer. Rather, it makes the need greater. Just as a man loves his wife all the time, but needs times to be with her, to foster and enrich the relationship, so Christians need definite times with the Lord when, like Moses, they are able to pray not only 'in the Spirit' but also 'face to face'.

Praying in the Spirit does not devalue the work of 'prayer chains' and the use of the telephone to share news and urge others to prayer. Our own church prayer chain, which operates both morning and evening, seeks to be submitted to the Spirit. The decision to join the prayer chain is only made after praying about it, and seeking the mind of the Spirit. As the requests are passed along the chain – the same written request or praise item is passed – so there is the need to make sure that what is being agreed in prayer is what the Holy Spirit would have people to pray.

Praying in the Spirit does not make prayer diaries and the use of prayer letters and prayer news invalid. I remember the former principal of a theological college saying that he was presented with so many requests for prayers and so many news letters that he couldn't cope with them all. He knew it was wrong and unnecessary to be guilt-ridden that he didn't pray for everything. His habit was to pray about what the Lord would have him pray about! He knew what he was to labour in prayer over, and he knew what he could leave to others.

Praying in the Spirit does not mean we neglect very practical aspects of prayer, such as choosing the best, quietest and warmest – or coolest – room in which to pray. After all, we are not disembodied spirits, and our bodies and minds have a real part to play in prayer. If we are not physically at ease, or our mind is distracted, we shall not find it easy to pray in the Spirit.

We do one another a disservice by insisting that we all pray in the same way in the Spirit. I believe the New Testament teaches that all can speak in tongues, that many do, and that none must. Some long to speak in tongues and do not. Some do, and then fail to use the gift that God has given to them, and it fades away. As Paul writes in 1 Corinthians 14.14–15: 'For if I pray in a tongue, my spirit prays, but my mind is unfruitful. So what shall I do? I will pray with my spirit, and I will also pray with my mind; I will sing with my spirit, but I will also sing with my mind.' There, quite clearly, the mind and the spirit are to act together, and this would usually be the situation in a corporate time of prayer. But when our mind is dull or uninformed or, dare I suggest, when our mind is sick or handicapped – why should we not expect a Christian to pray in tongues in the Spirit? (I write as a part-time chaplain to a hospital for mentally handicapped people. Their mouths may not be able to communicate much, but their eyes reflect the spiritual light within.)

We may experience that 'praying in the Spirit' is a seemingly unintelligent groan inwardly – as Paul writes in Romans 8.26–27. Jesus himself groaned inwardly in the Spirit when words were inadequate. For others, praying in the Spirit will be a marvellous inward release and overflow more in praise than petition.

This variety of experience is best stated in James Montgomery's hymn. Montgomery was one of the early hymn writers in the eighteenth-century evangelical revival of England. Up to that time it had been illegal to sing hymns! He lived in Sheffield just up the hill from where, nowadays, a very modern hospital and university stand. Had he lived today he would have been able to look out over the coal fields and steel mills of Yorkshire. He would have heard the roars of two large football grounds on a Saturday afternoon, and yet for men and women in every generation he has expressed something of praying in the Spirit.

Prayer is the soul's sincere desire,
Uttered or unexpressed;
The motion of a hidden fire
That trembles in the breast.

Prayer is the burden of a sigh,
The falling of a tear,
The upward glancing of an eye
When none but God is near.

Prayer is the simplest form of speech
That infant-lips can try,
Prayer the sublimest strains that reach
The Majesty on high.

Prayer is the contrite sinner's voice,
Returning from his ways,
While angels in their songs rejoice,
And cry, 'Behold, he prays!'

Prayer is the Christian's vital breath,
The Christian's native air,
His watchword at the gates of death:
He enters heaven with prayer.

Nor prayer is made by man alone,
The Holy Spirit pleads;
And Jesus, on the eternal throne,
For sinners intercedes.

O thou by whom we come to God,
The Life, the Truth, the Way,
The path of prayer thyself hast trod:
Lord, teach us how to pray![4]

A new discovery?

'Praying in the Spirit' is not theologically complicated, rather it is spiritually exciting. 'Prayer in the Spirit suggests new avenues waiting to be explored, new resources to be tapped and new power to be released.'[5]

For some Christians such praying is their experience

from the start of their new relationship with Christ. For others – and possibly for many – prayer is a real struggle and battle until they come to know the release, or fulness or baptism of the Spirit and then they 'take off'. That was the experience of Dr Samuel Chadwick, a former principal of Cliff College, the Methodist Home Missionary Training and Bible College. He described his spiritual experience in these words: 'The Baptism of the Spirit gave me a new joy and a new power, a new love and a new compassion. It gave me a new Bible and a new message. Above all else it gave me a new understanding and a new intimacy in the communion and ministry of prayer. It taught me to pray in the Spirit.'[6]

Fortunately it is not only Bible College principals for whom that is true. Many ordinary Christians – housewives, businessmen, young people at school or starting out at work – have experienced this new release and freedom in the Spirit. They have discovered, as one young person put it, that 'God blesses and uses us, not according to our merit, but according to His love'. They have also discovered a new depth, reality and meaning to praying in the Spirit, and a new desire to win their friends for Christ, and a new power through which to witness to them.

They may have come to a point in their Christian lives, where they could so easily have given it all up because their faith had become empty. God then met with them, baptised them in the Spirit and from then onwards they have grown in their understanding and practice of prayer in a way that has been a blessing to themselves and to many others. Prayer has come alive because they have discovered a deeper meaning to 'praying in the Spirit'.

Chapter Four: Notes

1. Andrew Murray *With Christ in the School of Prayer* (Nisbet, 1902) p. 201.
2. R. A. Torrey. *How to pray* (Oliphants, 1955) p. 58.

3. J. I. Packer. *Keep in step with the Spirit* (Inter-Varsity Press, Leicester, 1984) p. 79.
4. James Montgomery (1771–1854). In *Mission Praise* 190 (Marshalls, Basingstoke, 1983).
5. Arthur Wallis, *Pray in the Spirit* (Kingsway, Eastbourne, 1970) p. 6.
6. Samuel Chadwick, *The Path of Prayer* (Hodder & Stoughton, 1931).

Five: The World and Prayer

Colonel James Irwin is among the astronauts to have landed on the Moon. Reflecting on his experience he said: 'There is one thing more important than man walking on the Moon. That is that God has walked on the Earth.'

It is good to be reminded that Jesus of Nazareth actually walked the dusty roads and tracks of Palestine almost 2,000 years ago. Modern visitors to the Holy Land can walk in the steps of the Master, whether in Jerusalem, Nazareth, Galilee or the Jordan, and be reminded that our faith is concerned with heaven and earth. Jesus himself taught us to pray: 'Thy will be done on earth as it is in heaven.'

We cannot escape the fact that while prayer may take us to the very throne of God in heaven, we also live daily in the world. It may be the world of business, the university, the trades unions, the home, the school, the factory, the fields. It may be the world of bustling crowds or a secluded room. We are called to live in the world and to pray for the world. First we must understand what the Bible means by 'the world'. That will help us to understand why prayer can be a real struggle and also a glorious privilege.

The meaning of the 'world'

The word 'world' means different things. John, in his Gospel, uses it in at least three different ways.

(i) Firstly, he uses the word 'world' to describe *the created universe* and every part of it, however small, as well as the complete world system. 'The true light that gives light to every man was coming into the world. He was in the world, and though the world was made through him. . . .' (John 1.9–10).

(ii) Secondly, the 'world' refers to all *the people* who have lived, are living and will live on the face of the earth. 'God so loved the world that He gave His one and only Son that whoever believes in Him shall not perish but have eternal life' (John 3.16). One of the glorious prospects of heaven is to anticipate that people from every part of the world are going to be there: 'There before me was a great multitude that no-one could count, from every nation, tribe, people and language, standing before the throne and in front of the Lamb' (Rev. 7.9).

(iii) Thirdly, however, John uses the word 'world' to describe that system of values, standards, outlook and attitudes that will not accept God's rule, or submit to His authority. It is the world that has been *affected by the Fall*, marred by sin and broken by evil. It is the world referred to when Satan is described as the god of this world (2 Cor. 4.4). It is the world that did not recognise Jesus (John 1.10) and the world that will not have this man (the Lord) to reign over it (Luke 19.14).

Both John and James, in the New Testament, warn us that as Christians we have to choose between our love and commitment to God, and our compromise and friendship with this world:

> 'Do not love the world or anything in the world. If anyone loves the world, the love of the Father is not in him. For everything in the world – the cravings of sinful man, the lust of the eyes and the boasting of what he has and does – comes not from the Father but from the world. The world and its desires pass away, but the man who does the will of God lives for ever' (1 John 2.15–17).

'You adulterous people, don't you know that friendship with the world is hatred towards God? Anyone who chooses to be a friend of the world becomes an enemy of God' (Jas. 4.4).

It is most important that we grasp the meaning of the word 'world' so that we understand how 'the world' can affect our praying.

Let me put it another way. Jesus made the world as a *place*. Jesus deeply loves the *people* of the world, but sin and evil has marred and twisted the *practices* and *principles* of the world and debased what God has made.

Our relationship with the world

Faced with the world, what attitude are we to adopt to it? Jesus made his positive attitude abundantly clear when He was praying for His church in what we know as His Great High Priestly Prayer (John 17). There are three possible attitudes that the Christian can adopt.

(i) Firstly, we might decide *to withdraw* from the world. Christians have done this all down the ages. Some have been called to withdraw from the world to the discipline of a monastic life. For example, the Franciscan order, although withdrawn from the world, are very aware of what goes on in the world, and spend much time in prayer for the world. Yet they may not be free from the spirit of the world. Cardinal Basil Hume, addressing the monks of Ampleforth, said: 'In the life of any priest the two practices that tend first to be dropped are reading and prayer.'[1]

A modern form of isolation is for Christians to withdraw from all secular activity. They live for their church, work and home, but take no part in secular social activities. They regard politics as a dirty game which Christians should not get involved in. They will not read any books other than Christian ones, and they have no real friends who are not fellow-Christians. We are not disembodied spirits, and to live in holy huddles is a wrong attitude to the world, because it was not Jesus' attitude to the world: 'My prayer is not that you take them out of the world but that you protect them from the evil one' (John 17.15).

(ii) Secondly, we might decide that we must be *identified* with the world, to the point of becoming just like it, so that the world will accept us and listen to us. Such a view is illogical, personally disastrous and scripturally wrong. Why should the world take any notice of the Church and the Christian if they are no different? The world is described as 'darkness' while the Christian is to be like 'light' shining out in the darkness.

In the same prayer Jesus prayed: 'I have given them your word, and the world has hated them, for they are not of the world any more than I am of the world' (John 17.14).

One of the saddest stories in the New Testament concerns a man called Demas. He is only mentioned three times, but his story runs like this:

ACT ONE: 'Epaphras, my fellow-prisoner for Christ Jesus, sends you greetings. And so do Mark, Aristarcus, *Demas* and Luke, *my fellow-workers*' (Philem. 23–24).

ACT TWO: 'Our dear friend Luke, the doctor, and *Demas* send you greetings' (Col. 4.14).

ACT THREE: 'Do your best to come to me quickly, for *Demas*, *because he loved this world*, has *deserted me* and gone to Thessalonica' (2 Tim. 4.9).

What a sad decline and fall! The man who had fellowship with the apostle Paul, and was a travelling companion of Gospel-writer Luke, eventually succumbed to the pressures of the world. And his is not an isolated case!

I remember a young Christian man called Peter. He came from a good Christian home, and was converted when he was sixteen. While still at High School he belonged to the Christian fellowship and became a member of the committee. With the young people at church he would share in, and at times lead, the weekly Bible Study. Then came the time for him to go away to college. If you pressed him he would admit that he missed home and his Christian friends, but did his best to keep up his Christian life. Gradually he began to fall away. Other students stayed up much later than he was used to, and he began to stay up with them. Now he woke up only just in time to get to lectures, whereas previously he had insisted on reading his Bible and praying at the start of the day. He watched more TV and videos than he used to, and some he would have to admit were such that he would be ashamed if his parents and Christian friends knew. The edge had been taken off Peter's spiritual appetite. He found he had adopted standards and values, the use of time and money, and thought patterns that were increasingly determined by the values and practices of 'the world', and less and less by what would please the Lord. The Lord still loves him, but his love for the Lord has grown very weak, and his love for the world has taken over.

(iii) The third attitude we might take towards the world, and the right one, is to *influence* it for good and for God, rather than being influenced by it. 'As you sent me into the world, I have sent them into the world. For them I sanctify myself, that they too may be truly sanctified' (John 17.18–19). Or again, related to Jesus' final commission to His disciples: 'As the Father has sent me, I am sending you' (John 20.21). For Jesus that meant He took flesh, and became a man and lived among us. He became one of us in order to win the world back for God.

Praying for the world

You may well be wondering how all this talk about the 'world' affects our praying. Let me summarise what we have been saying and then I will show you.

We have done two things. We have tried to understand what 'the world' means, and then what the Christian's attitude should be towards the world.

We have said that 'the world' might refer to places, or to people, but often – and this is the part that affects our prayers very specially – to the principles and standards all around us. Our attitude and reaction to 'the world' might be to withdraw and be isolated. It might be to be like others in the world and be identified with it. Jesus teaches us that both of these are the wrong attitudes, and that we must seek positively to influence the world for God.

How do we do that, and how does it link up with prayer? We need to have three things:

(i) The spirit of prayer.
(ii) 'Time out' from the world.
(iii) A vision for the world.

(i) *The spirit of prayer* We live in a world of sophisticated television, video, radio, computers and electronic gadgets and wizardry of all sorts. Our forefathers would have been stunned to see colour television pictures relayed back from the moon. But, however far advanced our research and discovery may be, we still need to ensure that our receivers and sets are properly and finely tuned to hear or see the signals being transmitted. We still have to deal with problems of bad reception or interference. In the same way, the Christian has to make sure that he is not getting worldly interference in his spirit as he comes to pray.

St Paul put it this way: 'Do not conform any longer to the pattern of this world, but be transformed by the renewing of your mind. Then you will be able to test and approve what God's will is – His good, pleasing and perfect will' (Rom. 12.2).

Our minds and spirits are continually bombarded by the standards, sins and spirit of the world so we must take time 'tuning in' to the Lord when we come to pray. What does that mean in practice? It may mean for some that there has to be a time of confession and repentance because we know there are – and have been – sins of disobedience, unbelief and unwillingness in our lives, which have got to be put right with the Lord before our prayers can become a reality.

It may mean that we read some relevant part of the Bible before we pray, so that we are more sensitively tuned to the mind of God. It will certainly demand that we seek to open our lives to the influence and promptings of the Spirit of God. St Paul, writing in 1 Corinthians chapter two, explains why this is necessary. Our natural human mind will not think in the way that God by His Holy Spirit thinks, and therefore we would not naturally pray according to the mind of the Lord.

> 'The man without the Spirit does not accept the things that come from the Spirit of God for they are foolishness to him, and he cannot understand them, because they are spiritually discerned' (1 Cor. 2.14).

> 'We have not received the spirit of the world, but the Spirit who is from God, that we may understand what God has freely given us' (1 Cor. 2.12).

E. M. Bounds expressed that contrast between our natural spirit and the Holy Spirit when he wrote: 'Men of the world imagine prayer to be too impotent a thing to come into rivalry with business methods and worldly position.'[2] We all know that same tension and temptation. It is seemingly better to plan and work and have a meeting about a problem, rather than spend time in prayer seeking the Lord's will.

We had come to a position in our own church life

where we knew that we needed a fresh vision from the Lord. The Church leaders agreed, therefore, to set aside one week in the church calendar – at the beginning of a new year – to ask for the Lord's guidance. We focused upon this in our Sunday worship, we held ladies' prayer meetings during the day, a breakfast for men, an evening of prayer and a half-night of prayer, as well as smaller fellowship groups meeting together and individuals setting time aside for prayer.

The church members were asked to write to me, to share what they felt God had been impressing upon them during the week, either for themselves or for the church corporately. It was thrilling to discover that God had done so much among us. Some individual Christians found that God had made areas of Christian service clear to them. For the church as a whole God made clear what was to be the next step in our life together. We would never have come to that unity of vision through a committee or discussion. Often the spirit of the world can be in the church, even right at the centre, guiding the decisions. We need the Spirit of the Lord in the Church of the Lord.

If you liken the church to a ship, and the world to the sea, then it is disastrous if the spirit of the world gets into the church! Yet all too often this is what happens. For example, if a church council is a debating forum rather than a fellowship of praying people, they are in danger of sharing human, worldly wisdom, rather than discerning and discovering the mind of the Spirit (1 Cor. 2.6–16).

(ii) *'Time out' from the world* If the right spirit is essential for prayer, then sufficient time and opportunity for prayer is equally vital. The world rushes on from one thing to the next. Today's world is marked out by noise and activity, violence and a sense of competition and pressure. The Christian is called deliberately to separate himself from these pressures from time to time in order to pray. It is not a new situation, but every generation has to learn the truth. Jesus knew the very same pressures, and Mark tells us that 'Very early in the morning, while it was still dark, Jesus got up, left the house and went off to a solitary place, where He prayed' (Mark 1.35). At regular intervals in His ministry Jesus would withdraw into the mountains, or a quiet place, away from the crowds and the constant demands of people in order to make time for prayer with His Father. We also need to make time. Professor Hallesby writes:

> 'The child of God can grieve Jesus in no worse way than to neglect prayer. For by so doing he severs the connection between himself and the Saviour, and his inner life is doomed to be withered and crippled, as is the case with most of us.'[3]

Cardinal Hume tells us:

> 'We can have the attitude, for instance (unconscious I know), that we have the day to plan, all these activities in which we must engage, and then, somehow or other, prayer to be fitted in. Or we can have the attitude that we have prayers to say, and look upon the work we have to do as flowing from our prayer.'[4]

In a similar vein Paul Bilheimer writes:

> 'Satan's most successful strategy for the dilution of a ministry is to keep God's servant so occupied with reading, organisation, study, administration, visiting, putting out the fires of opposition and criticism that his devotional life is starved.'[5]

The lesson is simple for all of us – we must plan our prayer, and pray our plan. Nobody is going to give us time for prayer. We must have a will to pray, and a plan for prayer, and seek to work it out. Some people will be able to withdraw to their own room and literally shut the door for prayer. Others will have a favourite place where they like to go – it may be a church or outside somewhere where they are more able to tune into the Lord. Others, who cannot get physically alone that easily, can shut themselves in with the Lord within their minds and commune in their hearts with Him. Others, still, will find they have time and opportunity to pray when travelling in the train, or on the bus, or driving their car.

(iii) *A vision for the world* Here we reach the very heart of the matter. We are called to fulfil the ministry of praying for the world. The principles and powerful influence of the world may make prayer harder, but the people and places of the world make prayer more necessary.

God is looking for people who will pray on behalf of the world. Ezekiel writes: 'I (God) looked for a man among them who would build up the wall and stand before me in the gap on behalf of the land so that I would not have to destroy it, but I found none. So I will pour out my wrath on them and consume them with my fiery anger, bringing down on their own heads all they had done' (Ezekiel 22.30–31). We shall spend more time considering this vital ministry of intercession for the world (chapter 10), but just now we must notice that it is not a matter of praying for the world because we have nothing else to do, or nothing else we *can* do, but because it is God's way of influencing the world He has made. S. D. Gordon put it like this: 'The greatest thing anyone can do for God and for man is to pray. Prayer is striking the winning blow . . . service is gathering up the results.'[6]

John Wesley puts it strikingly in these words: 'God will do nothing but in answer to prayer.' In a way that we may not fully understand, the sovereign God has chosen to limit what He will do to the prayers and response of men.

Paul makes the same point, writing to his fellow worker Timothy. 'I urge, then, first of all, that requests, prayers, intercession and thanksgiving be made for everyone – for kings and all those in authority, that we may live peaceful and quiet lives in all godliness and holiness. This is good and pleases God our Saviour, who wants all men to be saved and to come to the knowledge of the truth' (1 Tim. 2.1–4).

Paul is connecting effective evangelism, a peaceful society, and the faithful prayers of the men together! This truth was vividly brought home to me a few years ago when it was my privilege and responsibility to be Chaplain to the Mayor (or First Citizen) of one of the London Boroughs. As Chaplain I had an official badge of office to wear. The chain bore the Coat of Arms of the Borough, which itself was backed by a Cross, under which was the motto of the Borough 'In Unity Progress'. It was a simple and clear illustration that behind everything has to be the message of the Cross, because God longs that all people should be saved, an end best achieved in a calm and peaceful society. Thus one of the prime responsibilities of the local authority, its council and officers is the peace, welfare and harmony of the citizens – and they come from a variety of cultural, religious and racial backgrounds. The work in the world has to be supported by prayer for the world.

Such work will be seen one day as the most important work we can do. Paul Bilheimer has written: 'When the books of heaven are opened it will be written for all to read that the pray-ers, and not the mayors, or kings or prime ministers or presidents are the real moulders of the world.'[7]

Such work is hard work, but God has given husbands and wives a mighty privilege in praying together for many aspects of this world's life. Yet, the tragedy is that few partners use that privilege. It may be that husbands and wives have not been taught to pray together. They may be shy of praying together. They may find it difficult to admit their need to each other – that they need to pray. What a blessing they miss out on.

Writing in his autobiography, Canon Harry Sutton,

the Canon Missioner of the South American Missionary Society, tells of the time he was taking part in a forum at a well-known Christian convention of several thousand people. 'One question asked was "Do the members of the panel find it easy or difficult to pray with their respective partner in marriage?" I found myself the only one of the panel who made a common practice of praying with my wife. I just could not understand how Christian folk could deny themselves such blessing. Praying with Olive has been one of the greatest strengths of our marriage and my ministry.'[8]

We need to ensure that we pray faithfully for the world in our church life. It is so easy to fall into the trap of praying for the local, personal and immediate, and forgetting the world-wide and on-going needs. Those of us who have the privilege of leading a congregation in prayer need to check that we are diligently praying for the world in its varied needs. Those who lead the church or fellowship times of prayer ought to ensure that we don't limit ourselves to the children's work and the Sunday School, and the financial needs, but bring in the main news stories covered by our responsible press and television.

As we bring to God, in prayer, all the concerns in our daily lives, the local needs, the national problems, and the international issues, so we shall find that we open all these situations to the influence of God's Spirit in a new and powerful way. We may never have the privilege of flying around the world, but our place of prayer will become for us the heart of the world from which we reach up to God with the prayer of faith. The places for which we pray may be separated from us by thousands of miles, but our prayers bring them under the influence of God's power and concern. Prayer is the decisive factor in the affairs of the world. The world of prayer can change the people of the world.

Chapter Five: Notes

1. Basil Hume, *In Search for God* (SPCK, 1977) p. 135.
2. E. M. Bounds, *The Weapon of Prayer* (Baker Book House, 1979) p. 56.
3. O. Hallesby, *Prayer* (Inter Varsity Fellowship, 1948) p. 29.
4. Basil Hume, op. cit., p. 119.
5. Paul Bilheimer, *Destined to Overcome* (Kingsway, Eastbourne, 1982) p. 59.
6. S. D. Gordon, *Quiet Talks on Prayer* (Revell, New York, 9th edition) p. 19.
7. Paul Bilheimer, op. cit., p. 55.
8. Harry Sutton, *You'll never walk alone* (Marshalls, Basingstoke, 1984) p. 152.

Six: Overcoming the Flesh – The Practice

I don't find it easy to pray, and I'm sure that is true for most Christians. The difficulties are well known. We are either too tired, or too rushed. We may find it hard to put aside all our activities and be quiet. Our minds wander off to a whole list of other things we could be doing. At other times the telephone, the family, or people knocking at the door whittle away the time we have set aside for prayer. If prayer becomes too hard, we may take the 'spiritual' way out and pretend that we are in an attitude of prayer all the time and therefore obeying the instruction: 'Pray at all times'. So we think we don't need to worry about a special time for prayer and, very soon, the well guarded time for prayer has become shorter and then almost non-existent.

What's the *real* problem? We need to remember that when we come to pray, we are challenging the world, the flesh and the devil. Having considered 'the world', I now want to focus upon 'the flesh' and how it affects our prayer lives.

Writing to the Christians at Rome, Paul said:

> 'For those who live according to the flesh set their minds on the things of the flesh, but those who live according to the Spirit set their minds on the things of the Spirit. . . . But you are not in the flesh, you are in the Spirit, if the Spirit of God really dwells in you' (Rom. 8.5, 9, RSV).

The 'flesh' is not our body and blood and muscle –

our physical body – but our sinful nature. A simple way to understand and remember what FLESH is, is to write the word backwards and cancel the first letter – i.e. ~~H~~ SELF.

If any of the 'self' words get into our praying, then we have problems. Praying must not become self-centred, self-confident, self-important, self-interested, full of self-pity, or self-righteousness, self-willed and self-seeking. 'Self' can be 'the little tin god', 'the idol' in our lives, 'what is good' for me. Self, or 'the flesh' is the great hindrance we face in prayer.

The Bible teaches various ways by which we can overcome this hindrance and I want to list them for us so that we find our practice of prayer being effective. We need to have:

One. The right motive for prayer

Two verses make the point simply and clearly: 'Ask and it will be given to you; seek and you will find; knock and the door will be opened to you. For everyone who asks receives; he who seeks finds; and to him who knocks, the door will be opened' (Matt. 7.7–8). 'You do not have, because you do not ask God. When you ask, you do not receive because you ask with wrong motives, that you may spend what you get on your pleasures' (Jas. 4.2–3). There are two very clear illustrations of this in the Bible.

Elijah on Mount Carmel (1 Kings 18) During a time of spiritual decline in Israel, Elijah the prophet challenged King Ahab to a trial of spiritual strength. The 450 prophets of Baal and Elijah were both to take a bull, cut it in pieces and put it on an altar of wood and then call on their respective gods or God to consume the sacrifice by fire. Whichever god answered by fire was to be seen as the true God. To make matters more difficult for himself Elijah had his wooden altar drenched with water. It was obviously a matter of great personal honour and concern that God answered Elijah's prayer, and we read in verses 36–37: 'At the time of the sacrifice, the prophet Elijah stepped forward and prayed: "O LORD, God of Abraham, Isaac and Israel, let it be known today that you are God in Israel and that I am your servant and have done all these things at your command. Answer me, O LORD, answer me, so these people will know that you, O LORD, are God, and that you are turning their hearts back again." Then the fire of the LORD fell and burned up the sacrifice. . .'

Even Elijah wasn't entirely free from the temptation to get in on the act and gain some credit for himself. It was not until he was concerned solely that people should know that God was God that the fire fell.

The mother of James and John (Matthew 20.21) 'Grant that one of these two sons of mine may sit at your right hand and the other at your left in your kingdom.' It is very natural for a mother to want the best for her sons but her motive seems to have been wrong. It is not always easy to untangle our motives when praying for ourselves or others. It is hard to be completely disinterested. For example, when we are praying that Grandma will be free from her arthritis, are we praying this for God's glory, for Grandma's peace or for our sakes – that she will be less irritable? Again, when we pray that our children will marry Christians, are we motivated by God's will, their blessing or the fact that it will save us parents many future worries? Self can be so subtle, but very real.

It is a problem we may face when praying with others, not only when we are praying alone. The prayer group or meeting is not free from those who are quite pleased with what they have done as Christians, or the 'up-to-date news' they have to share, and it is a temptation to show off and blow our own trumpets so that others might know what good Christians we are!

Some Christians err in the other direction, and feel it wrong to pray for themselves and their personal needs at all. While I have deliberately not devoted a separate chapter to 'petition', may I say as clearly as I can that Jesus tells us to pray for ourselves and our own needs. It is there in the Lord's Prayer as we speak about our daily bread, our spiritual weakness and our failure in the past. It is there, also, in the Sermon on the Mount, as Jesus tells us very clearly to 'Ask and it will be given to you; seek and you will find; knock and the door will be opened to you. . . . . how much more will your Father in heaven give good gifts to those who ask Him!' (Matt. 7.7, 11).

Two. A pure heart

'Blessed are the pure in heart, for they will see God' (Matt. 5.8). A pure heart and spirit is one that is free from any conscious and deliberate sin. It means there is no unconfessed sin in our lives.

'Surely the arm of the LORD is not too short to save, nor his ear too dull to hear. But your iniquities have separated you from your God; your sins have hidden his face from you, so that he will not hear' (Isa. 59.1–2).

'If I had cherished sin in my heart, the Lord would not have listened; but God has surely listened and heard my voice in prayer. Praise be to God who has not rejected my prayer or withheld his love from me!' (Ps. 66.18–20).

Confession in prayer is covered more fully in a later chapter; just for the moment we need to see that purity of heart relates both to the present and the past. For example, King David has been involved in a whole catalogue of sins – covetousness, greed, adultery and murder – and it was not until he had brought these out into the open and confessed them before God that he knew he was clean inwardly (Ps. 51.3–12; 2 Samuel 11). Sin will not only make prayer very hard, but it will dull the desire we have to pray, and possibly bring prayer to a complete halt.

The people of Isaiah's day were bringing their prayers and offering their religious fasts to the Lord, but nothing was happening. God had to teach them that so long as they had wrong attitudes to Himself, to their neighbours and those in need He would not hear and answer their prayers. They needed hearts that were pure before God and before men.

Purity of heart doesn't only relate to our relationship with God, or our attitudes to our neighbours and ourselves. It can also refer to the attitudes we have towards possessions. Ezekiel tells us about some of the leaders of Israel who came to him expecting some word from the Lord: 'Then the word of the Lord came to me: "Son of man, these men have set up idols in their hearts and put wicked stumbling-blocks before their faces. Should I let them enquire of me at all?" ' (Ezek. 14.2–3). They had set up idols in their hearts and an idol is anything that we think is more important than the Lord.

If, when we come to pray, we find the same person, problem, or subject coming into our minds and occupying the limelight that should be reserved for the Lord, then that is the idol we must deal with if we would be pure in heart.

Three. Forgiving others

If there is one requirement that Jesus mentioned more than any other it is this one: 'Therefore, if you are offering your gift at the altar and there remember that your brother has something against you, leave your gift there in front of the altar. First go and be reconciled to your brother; then come and offer your gift' (Matt. 5.23–24).

'If you forgive men when they sin against you, your heavenly Father will also forgive you. But if you do not forgive men their sins, your Father will not forgive your sins' (Matt. 6.14–15).

'Then Peter came to Jesus and asked "Lord, how many times shall I forgive my brother when he sins against me? Up to seven times?" Jesus answered, "I tell you, not seven times, but seventy-seven times." ' Jesus went on to tell the parable of the unmerciful servant and ended: 'This is how my heavenly Father will treat each of you unless you forgive your brother from your heart' (Matt. 18.21–35).

We have the same thought repeated elsewhere in the New Testament: 'I want men everywhere to lift up holy hands in prayer, without anger or disputing' (1 Tim. 2.8). These passages are not all saying exactly the same thing. There is the distinction between whether someone has sinned against us, and we need to forgive them, and whether we have caused someone else to stumble and sin and we need to put that right.

The need to forgive and be forgiven is deep rooted. Forgiveness means lifting off a burden. Forgiveness is someone else lifting off from us a load we are carrying. God made that possible when Jesus died on the Cross. John Bunyan (in *The Pilgrim's Progress*) tells the story of Christian coming to the Cross and finding his burden roll off his back towards the foot of the Cross to disappear from sight for ever. We may need to forgive and lift burdens off other people.

Some people are still carrying in their lives fear or guilt from past years. We have heard of mature adults who when they were children were shut out in the cold for some small disobedience, who have felt neglected and hurt and who have carried that scar and resentment for years. They need to forgive someone. A parent may have walked out of the family home years ago, causing great hurt, and now find themselves full of guilt and needing to be forgiven by others. Sadly, such stories are not unusual. Forgiveness may relate to something that happened years ago – in the family, a 'tiff' between lovers, a row at the office, a disagreement between two members of the church, or a church member and the pastor. Your fellowship both with God and with Christians will be affected by such incidents.

This need to forgive is the only part of the Lord's Prayer which Jesus amplified (Matthew 6.14–15). He wanted to make sure that we got the point He was making. It was inconsistent to ask God to forgive us when we were not willing to forgive others. It meant that we hadn't understood the spirit of forgiveness which God shows to us, and it also revealed that we were being two-faced and double-minded. We wanted God to be merciful to us, but we were not willing and ready to be merciful to others.

The spirit of unforgiveness is so often the barrier that dams the flow of God's power and love in our lives. It can be likened to a great Canadian river that freezes over in the cold weather, thus trapping the logs the water is supposed to carry down. Each log might be a picture of some obstacle or relationship that needs forgiveness and it is trapped by the icy waters of a cold and unloving spirit. The streams of God's power will flow again only when the ice has been melted and the logs have been dealt with. If you thaw the ice, then you will remove the log jam. Didn't Jesus have something to say about the specks in other people's eyes, and the logs in our own?

One verse that speaks about forgiveness (Mark 11.26) also speaks about our next condition.

Four. A believing heart

' "Have faith in God," Jesus answered. "I tell you the truth, if anyone says to this mountain, 'Go, throw yourself into the sea,' and does not doubt in his heart but believes that what he says will happen, it will be done for him. Therefore I tell you, whatever you ask for in prayer, believe that you have received it, and it will be yours." ' (Mark 11.22–24).

John has some very similar promises about asking for anything in prayer in his Gospel (John 14.14; 15.15; and 16.23) and we have talked about these in the chapter about praying in the name of Jesus.

When it comes to that very difficult subject of praying for healing James writes: 'Is any one of you sick? He should call for the elders of the church to pray over him and anoint him with oil in the name of the Lord. And the prayer offered in faith will make the sick person well; the Lord will raise him up. If he has sinned, he will be forgiven. Therefore confess your sins to each other and pray for each other so that you may be healed. The prayer of a righteous man is poweful and effective' (Jas. 5.14–16).

Praying in faith for those who are sick is not a simple matter. Others have written fully and helpfully on the subject,[1] and I will only make two points about praying in faith.

(i) The Greek language has different words for our one English word to 'heal'. One Greek word means to heal physically, and, interestingly, that is the word used in Matthew 8.16–17 and in 1 Peter 2.24: 'By his wounds you have been healed'. Another Greek word means 'to be made whole' and describes salvation as relating to every part of our being and nature. That is the word used in James: 'That you may be healed.' James is therefore saying that when we pray in faith – whatever the needs – the Lord will answer and there will be healing and blessing of some kind whether or not the person lives or dies.

In 1984 I was able to visit Canon Jim Glennon in Australia and attend one of the famous healing services which have been a feature of the Wednesday evenings in Sydney Cathedral for more than twenty years. I was troubled about this promise of the prayer of faith, when clearly people didn't always get better, and was so helped by Jim Glennon's reply. His testimony over those twenty years was that they had never not had blessing of one kind or another – either to the sick person or those who prayed for them. The night I was there, more than 500 people packed into the Cathedral. Ordinary men and women – trained and appointed – were those who prayed the prayer of faith. It was a memorable and moving experience.

(ii) If that is the prayer of faith as it relates especially to healing, I need to say more about it generally, for it is an abused and misunderstood condition that has caused some to make shipwreck of their faith. People tend to read Mark 11.24 like this: 'If I really believe that I'm going to receive what I have asked for, then I shall get it.' So the question is: Can I believe that one thousand pounds will drop through my letter box tomorrow because I need it to pay my bills? Can I believe that the sun will shine throughout my holiday because I need a real rest having been under much pressure? We are tempted to screw up our faith, pump up our hopes and convince ourselves that what we believe, we shall receive. It seems to me that some Christians actually pray in this way, and that is not what Jesus is teaching.

We can clearly and unreservedly pray on the basis of what God has said and promised in the Bible. For what God has said in His word, is the revelation of His will.

Some years ago I visited a coffee plantation in Kenya. Wherever I looked small coffee bushes were growing on the hillsides. When I asked the manager how many plants there were, he replied 'Some three thousand, five hundred.' Someone who has worked it out reckons that the Bible contains about three thousand five hundred promises. Just like the coffee plantation – wherever you look in the Scriptures will be God's promises. And it is those promises that give us the firm foundation on which we rest our hopes and prayers.

Probably the supreme example of living by faith is Abraham. God had promised to him and Sarah that, although they possessed no land and no son and were both too old to have children, He would bless them and make them a blessing and a mighty nation. It was to be twenty-five years before Isaac was born, but Paul, writing about this, says that Abraham did not waver in his faith: 'Against all hope, Abraham in hope believed and so became the father of many nations, just as it had been said to him, "So shall your offspring be." Without weakening in his faith, he faced the fact that his body was as good as dead – since he was about a hundred years old – and that Sarah's womb was also dead. Yet he did not waver through unbelief regarding the promise of God, but was strengthened in his faith and gave glory to God, being fully persuaded that God had power to do what he had promised' (Rom. 4.18–21).

Abraham's faith was like a muscle – the more he used it, the stronger it became. It is often here that we have practical problems. We need to learn to pray according to the measure of our faith. We may believe in theory that God can do this and that, but when it comes to practice, we are not so sure. We have to ask ourselves what we really believe God will do. In some ways we are back to the mountain in Mark 11 when Jesus said that if we believed we could remove mountains. This picture leads most of us to expect to see a mountain take off on some airborne carpet and land 'plop' in the sea. There is another way! Removing the mountain little by little, shovelful by shovelful.

David Pawson tells the story of a friend who was praying for the conversion of his neighbour and wondered why nothing happened. When the friend was asked if he thought God could work in his neighbour's life (whom the friend really didn't know) he had to admit his unbelief. The friend was trying to remove the mountain in one go. He had to learn to pray within his faith. What could he believe for? Taking a step at a time he could believe that he and his neighbour would begin talking to each other, then that the neighbour would invite himself and his wife into their home socially, and then that the neighbour would raise the question of religion, then that the neighbour would be willing to come to his church, and finally that the neighbour would respond to the preaching of the gospel. Taken in stages the mountain was moved. The neighbour trusted Christ and the friend learned a very important lesson about steps in faith. Pray within your faith.

Five. Keep close to Jesus

We need to keep close to Jesus – or to abide in Him, as the New Testament puts it. Satan would love to knock us off course, or to trip us up, and so Jesus knew how essential it is for us to abide in Him.

'I am the vine; you are the branches. If a man remains in me and I in him, he will bear much fruit; apart from me you can do nothing. . . . If you remain (abide) in me and my words remain in you, ask whatever you wish, and it will be given you' (John 15.5,7).

It is the close relationships at home, at work or at church which can be the greatest blessing or the areas that Satan attacks. Take marriage and the family, for example. Peter writes: 'Husband, in the same way be considerate as you live with your wives, . . . so that nothing will hinder your prayers' (1 Peter 3.7). It can be the little misunderstanding, the wrong reaction, and the misjudged feeling that brings tensions into a marriage, sometimes from within the home and sometimes from outside.

Like many other students, I am indebted to a godly minister in Oxford who taught us to 'keep short accounts with God and with one another'. Keeping close to Jesus is vital. One consequence of keeping close to Jesus is not to be unequally yoked together in partnership with unbelievers. 'What do righteousness and wickedness have in common? Or what fellowship can light have with darkness? What harmony is there between Christ and Belial? What does a believer have in common with an unbeliever?' (2 Cor. 6.14–15). This injunction certainly applies to the Christian considering the possibility of marriage to a non-Christian. You are commanded not to do so. It will also apply, in certain situations, to our work. For example, while a Christian may have no problems in being a *member* of a board where the majority are not Christians, I am sure that the same Christian would be wrong to set up in business on *equal terms* with an unbeliever.

We are called to be yoked with Jesus (Matt. 11.29) and so we cannot be yoked to those who don't follow Jesus, otherwise we shall find ourselves constantly pulled in two directions. One of the first areas of our life to suffer will be the life of prayer. We shall experience the pull and tension between the flesh (self) and the Spirit that Paul mentioned in Romans 8.

Keeping close to Jesus is something we have to work at. And prayer is something we have to work at. There has to be a mark of perseverance. Therefore –

Six. Keep on praying

That may sound strange to us when we can rejoice in and thrill at those times when the spirit of prayer has been flowing out and upwards and prayer has been unending and we have not wanted to stop. We thought we had prayed for five minutes and found it was an hour. Yes, there are those times when prayer is just like the eagle. We have allowed the Holy Spirit to carry us up to the heights and then just as the eagle rests its wings on the wind currents and allows the air to carry it along effortlessly, so our prayer has been borne along by the Spirit wherever He would lead us. That is true. It is also true that there are times when we need to persevere.

Jesus taught that men should always pray and not give up, and told the parable of the widow who kept on coming to the judge to vindicate her of her enemy. Finally, the judge yielded to the widow so that she would not eventually wear him out. Jesus' comment was: 'Listen to what the unjust judge says. And will not God bring about justice for His chosen ones, who cry out to him day and night? Will he keep putting them off? I tell you, he will see that they get justice, and quickly.

However, when the Son of Man comes, will he find faith on the earth?' (Luke 18.1–8).

Persistence in prayer is not the same as vain repetition. It is not the Christian equivalent of the prayer wheel, or the incantations of meditation, or the beads of the rosary.

There are occasions when we have to wrestle in prayer. We need to keep on praying – not because God has not heard, or has not promised to answer, but because we are involved in a spiritual battle and the enemy of prayer is holding up the answer. 'Do not be afraid, Daniel. Since the first day that you set your mind to gain understanding and to humble yourself before God, your words were heard, and I have come in response to them. But the prince of the Persian kingdom resisted me twenty-one days' (Dan. 10.12–13).

Our forefathers in the faith used to talk about 'praying through' until the answer came – whether it was for the conversion of a friend, a financial need to be met, a Christian worker to complete the work in hand, for revival to come or a church to be blessed.

Jesus 'prayed through' in Gethsemane (Matt. 26.43–44). The early church prayed for Peter's release from prison (Acts 12.5). Elijah prayed for the coming of rain (1 Kgs. 18) and we often pray together for industrial disputes to be settled, for hostages to be released, for a child to be healed and for guidance to be given. I suspect that we are more in danger of stopping too soon, than of carrying on too long when it comes to prayer.

Seven. Generous giving

There seems to be a vital link between effective praying and generous giving. It was said of George Müller of Bristol that he was a mighty man of prayer because he was a mighty giver. The Bible makes the same point: 'If a man shuts his ears to the cry of the poor, he too will cry out and not be answered' (Proverbs 21.13).

'All the believers were one in heart and mind. No-one claimed that any of his possessions was his own, but they shared everything they had. With great power the apostles continued to testify to the resurrection of the Lord Jesus, and much grace was with them all' (Acts 4.32–33).

There is, I am sure, a vital link between spiritual power and the proper attitude to material possessions. The materially rich western church is often spiritually impoverished when it comes to prayer. It is the Third World that is often able to teach us the spirit of utter dependence upon the Lord both in life generally and prayer particularly.

If we ask the question 'Who best demonstrates these conditions of praying rightly for God's glory, praying from a pure heart, being willing and able fully to forgive others, fully trusting and believing God for all things, keeping in very close fellowship with His heavenly Father, who was able to pray through to the end, and did so with a full and generous heart?' then we can come up with only one answer – and that is the Lord Jesus.

In all things He is our example and inspiration. It is 'in His name' we pray. It is 'in His Spirit' that we find reality as we pray. When we allow self or the flesh to dominate then we have trouble. But when we allow the spirit of Jesus to direct and inspire our prayers then we begin to find the reality and fruitfulness that Jesus said would be ours.

Chapter Six: Note

1. Among the most helpful books on healing are those by Canon Jim Glennon and Father Francis MacNutt.

Seven: Victory over Satan

Since we know that the Holy Spirit helps us in our weakness, and that His ministry is to give us joy and blessing when we pray, why do most of us still find it hard to get down to prayer? We face inner distractions, wandering thoughts and a strange restlessness in our spirit, and we are willing to do almost anything other than what we know we should be doing – and want to do – namely pray! Why?

Prayer brings us into the centre of the spiritual battle that is constantly waged between the 'flesh' and the spirit and between the Lord Jesus and Satan. There are two Kingdoms locked in unceasing conflict over the world – the Kingdom of God on the one hand, and the Kingdom of the Prince of this world, Satan, on the other.

There is a spiritual battle

Not every Christian is sure that there is such a person as Satan, or the devil, or consequently that there is a real spiritual battle. Isn't Satan someone we have invented to explain where evil came from? Might he not be just a rather unpleasant character from medieval paintings or William Blake's lurid drawings?

The Bible tells us, without any doubt and from almost the first page of the Bible, that Satan does exist. He is there as the serpent in the Garden of Eden (Gen. 3.1–5). I remember a fascinating conversation I had with two senior Christian men working for the BBC – one working in TV and the other in radio. They pointed out to me that God asked all the right questions – Who? What?

Why? Where? – and made Adam and Eve give the right answers. Satan, on the other hand, made the evasive comment, and latched onto the half-truth, sowing doubt, rather than broadcasting the truth; and this battle to communicate truth, or lies and half-truths has gone on ever since. It reminds us that we live in a world which is the battle ground of a spiritual struggle.

Jesus himself taught most about Satan. He experienced to the full his fierce and unrelenting attacks – in his temptations in the wilderness, through friend and enemy alike. It was Satan who believed he had scored the ultimate victory when Jesus was killed upon the Cross but, as we shall see, that apparent victory was to be turned into a crushing and lasting defeat for Satan.

Though mortally wounded and robbed of his power, Satan is still around. He attacked believers in the early church (Acts 5.1) and he goes on struggling against God and His purposes. But John records his downfall:

> 'And there was war in heaven. Michael and his angels fought against the dragon, and the dragon and his angels fought back. But he was not strong enough, and they lost their place in heaven. The great dragon was hurled down – that ancient serpent called the devil or Satan, who leads the whole world astray. He was hurled to the earth, and his angels with him. Then I heard a loud voice in heaven say: "Now have come the salvation and the power and the kingdom of our God, and the authority of His Christ. For the accuser of our brothers, who accuses them before our God day and night has been hurled down. They overcame him by the blood of the Lamb and by the Word of their testimony, they did not love their lives so much as to shrink from death" ' (Rev. 12.7–11).

Having read of the spiritual struggle in the Old Testament and seen its consequences in the life of Jesus and in heaven itself, we should not be surprised to find that Christians today throughout the world face a spiritual struggle. Nor is it surprising to find this struggle sharply focused in prayer. The good news is that we also read in the Scriptures that Satan was defeated by the Saviour when He died on the Cross and when He was raised from the dead. We can, therefore, have victory over Satan in our lives and in prayer.

The writers of the New Testament tell us in simple and straightforward words that we have a battle to fight.

> 'Finally, be strong in the Lord and in His mighty power. Put on the full armour of God, so that you can take your stand against the devil's schemes. For our struggle is not against flesh and blood, but against the rulers, against the authorities, against the powers of this dark world and against the spiritual forces of evil in the heavenly realms' (Paul, in Eph. 6.10–12).

> 'Your enemy the devil prowls around like a roaring lion looking for someone to devour. Resist him, standing firm in the faith' (1 Pet. 5.8–9).

> 'Submit yourselves, then, to God. Resist the devil and he will flee from you' (Jas. 4.7).

You may be a very young Christian, and for the first time in your life you are aware of temptations, of difficulties and of a spiritual battle in a way that is new. Don't worry. Up until now Satan has not bothered with you. You were quietly spiritually asleep in his kingdom. When Christ rescued you from the dominion of darkness and brought you into the kingdom of God and Jesus showed you His love and assured you of the forgiveness of sin, Satan was angry.

You may be a Christian who is actively serving your Lord. You have taught a Bible Class or given your testimony one day, only to find that you lose your temper or fall into sin the very next day. The day of blessing has been followed by the day of testing. You should not be surprised. That is what happened to Jesus. Following

His baptism by John the Baptist, the coming of the Spirit, and God's voice from heaven assuring Him of God's love and blessing at the start of His public ministry, He is then driven into the wilderness, alone and hungry, to be tested and tempted by Satan for forty days. Jesus was tempted and did no sin. It is not wrong to be tempted and to taste the spiritual battle.

You may be a senior missionary and know the spiritual battle in various ways: constant ill health, persistent discouragement, a nagging sense of failure in God's service, tensions and personality clashes within the missionary team and with the local church. You find it hard to love the Lord, let alone love the work He has called you to. May I gently remind you of the reality of the spiritual battle.

We are never going to be free of the conflict with Satan this side of the grave, but we can always rejoice in the conquest over Satan. We have the victory!

In the Name of Jesus
We have the victory.
In the Name of Jesus
Demons will have to flee.
Who can tell what God can do?
Who can tell of His love for you?
In the name of Jesus, Jesus,
We have the victory.
(Author unknown)

Victory in the spiritual battle

It is essential that we know the reality which that song expresses. We must not only sing it with our lips, but rejoice in the truth in our hearts and minds. Why and how do we have the victory in and through praise and prayer?

There are two great, unchanging spiritual truths we must grasp. The first is that we have victory through the work of the Lord Jesus on the Cross, and the second is that we have victory through our union with Jesus, risen from the dead, day by day.

I'll share with you, in a moment, the tactics of Satan who, although he is defeated utterly, won't lie down, but we must take into our hearts and minds the biblical basis for our victory in the spiritual struggle and therefore victory in prayer.

Victory through the Cross of Jesus

The New Testament tells us in no uncertain terms that Christ won the ultimate victory over Satan when He died on the Cross. Every time Satan believed he had won the battle against Jesus, he was shown to be wrong.

When Satan tried to tempt Jesus in the wilderness, the Lord determined to obey and trust His heavenly Father and His word completely (Matt. 4.1–11).

When Jesus died on the Cross, and took the sin of the whole world upon Himself, He pulled from under Satan's feet the very ground upon which he (Satan) was planning to attack us. It was Satan's plan to accuse us about our sin, guilt and failure. But when Jesus took all the evidence (i.e. sin and guilt and failure) that Satan intended to use against us, and nailed it to the Cross, then Satan had no case to bring against us (Col. 2.14).

The next stage of Satan's plan – if he couldn't win where sin was concerned – was to make us afraid of death. On the Cross, Jesus robbed death of its sting and power. He took away the *fear* of death through His death and resurrection.

As Paul writes in 1 Corinthians 15 – a passage that is often read at funeral services – ' "Death has been swallowed up in victory." "Where, O death is your victory? Where, O death, is your sting?" The sting of death is sin, and the power of sin is the law. But thanks be to God! He gives us the victory through our Lord Jesus Christ' (v. 5–7). Again we read: 'Jesus shared in their humanity so that by His death He might destroy him who holds the power of death – that is, the devil – and free those who all their lives were held in slavery by their fear of death' (Heb. 2.14–15).

I recall two men in the North of England – both fine Christians. There is a tradition in Yorkshire of 'Whit walks'. The whole church, including the children of the Sunday Schools, the uniformed organisations, the banners, and, if possible, the bands, would walk around the parish. We would stop two or three times, sing a couple of popular hymns and ask someone to give their testimony. The first man, Jack, clearly testified that one of the differences that Christ made to his life was that 'he was no longer afraid to die'.

Crossing over the pennines and moving from Yorkshire to Lancashire I recall a second man, a business man, who was rushed unexpectedly into hospital for a major operation. He faced the future – the possible separation from his wife with whom he had served the Lord so faithfully – quite unafraid. 'Sudden death – sudden glory' was his hope and faith.

Satan, at that point where he binds so many in fear, has truly been overcome and destroyed – the word literally means 'emptied of his power'. To use a military analogy, Satan is no longer issued with 'live ammunition' that can spiritually kill. He is only able to fight the war with 'dummy bullets', or 'blank cartridges'.

Paul sums up this glorious reality for us in Colossians 2 verses 13–15: 'Christ forgave us all our sins, having cancelled the written code, with its regulations, that was against us and that stood opposed to us; he took it away, nailing it to the cross. And having disarmed the powers and authorities, he made a public spectacle of them, triumphing over them by the cross.'

John has the same truth: 'The reason the Son of God appeared was to destroy the devil's work' (1 John 3.8).

The Christian church needs to learn again this first truth of victory over Satan. When Jesus died on the Cross and rose again He destroyed all the works of Satan. Whenever, therefore, we remind Satan about the victory of Jesus, through His blood shed on the Cross, once for all, Satan has to run away in fear and cower. The devil cannot bear to hear the name of Jesus lifted high. He cannot stand being reminded of the power of the shed blood on the Cross.

Paul Bilheimer puts it like this: 'Because of Christ's dynamic victory through the Cross and Resurrection we are Satan's masters. He can lord it over us no more. Instead of him having power over us, we have been given authority over him. This is the meaning of "enthronement with Christ".'[1]

Heirs with Christ

That leads us on to the second great truth we must grasp – we have victory through our union with Jesus, risen from the dead, day by day. It seems to me that many Christians have either missed or not understood this vital point. We have the victory in the battle not only because Christ conquered Satan on the Cross, but also because we are united with Christ in that victory by faith.

Twice in his letter to the Church at Ephesus, Paul reminds them that they – and we – are seated with Christ (Eph. 1.20; 2.6). Not only is Christ on the throne, but we share that position with Him. He alone is the King, and we are still His subjects and servants, but we share His victory.

Paul uses another more familiar picture in Romans 8 verse 17: 'Now if we are children, then we are heirs – heirs of God and co-heirs with Christ, if indeed we share in His sufferings in order that we may also share in His glory.' We were reminded earlier that the first key to prayer is becoming children of God through faith in Christ. That isn't the end of the story because we are children, we are also heirs. We are heirs of Christ's inexhaustible spiritual resources in His name. We have got to claim them and use them.

Let me explain: a husband and wife may have a joint deposit account, but they will both have to sign to draw on what is in it. One signature is not sufficient without the other. When we become joint-heirs with Christ it is as if God is making us a joint signatory of heaven's spiritual riches with Jesus. He has already signed His name – when He died and rose again. We now need to claim personally those riches for ourselves.

Many of us are living spiritually empty and bankrupt lives, powerless against sin, and ineffective in prayer, when we don't need to.

We shall need to use our inheritance with Christ because, although Satan is defeated, he is still a subtle and wily foe, and we should do well to study how he tries to make life and prayer especially difficult for us.

The tactics Satan uses

Satan is given many different names in the Bible, and each one tells us something about the tactics he uses and the way he works.

(i) Satan means adversary. He will oppose all that God wants to do, and he attacks Christians when they become spiritually alive. How does that relate to prayer? Often through Satan trying to delay answers to prayers and causing Christians to give up praying too soon.

'Do not be afraid, Daniel. Since the first day that you set your mind to gain understanding and to humble yourself before your God, your words were heard, and I have come in response to them. but the prince of the Persian kingdom resisted me twenty-one days' (Dan. 10.12–13).

Satan enlisted one of his spiritual allies to oppose Daniel and delay the answer to his prayer. God wasn't reluctant to answer, and Daniel needed to go on praying. We have seen the need to persevere in the Spirit, and that is because of Satan's work of opposition.

(ii) Devil means accuser. 'The accuser of our brothers, who accuses them before our God day and night. . .' (Rev. 12.10). The devil goes around spreading gossip, misunderstandings, slander, making us irritable or resentful towards others in the family or the fellowship. He makes one Christian afraid that another Christian is 'getting ahead of them', being given more attention. He sows jealousy. On the other hand he may make us feel guilty or depressed and introspective. His special weapon is to make Christians believe they have committed the unforgivable sin against the Holy Spirit. (Anyone who is *worried* about having committed the unforgivable sin has not committed it.) He has the cheek to accuse God to us, and tries to tell us that God doesn't love us, or that God is going to make unreasonable demands upon us.

It is not easy to pray when we have these feelings and thoughts going on in our minds. Once we realise what Satan is doing, we can quickly have the answer, but we need to be aware of his methods.

(iii) 'Apollyon' is a rare, but important, title for our adversary (Rev. 9.11). It means the destroyer. It is ironic that the one who has been destroyed by Jesus dares to parade around with that title. How can Satan destroy us? He may use illness, he may divide us from the fellowship or tell us that we don't need to go. He may turn us into workaholics with overwork or fear. He may tempt us with immorality or crime to break us up – and others with us.

(iv) The Father of Lies (John 8.44) was Jesus' name for Satan. (He is a forger and a counterfeit.) It is the oldest trick in the book, but it caught out Adam and Eve. 'Has God said?' He used it against Ananias and Sapphira (Acts 5) and he uses it against us – will God provide, guide, forgive, keep his promises? No wonder that we need to take the word of God – the Sword of the Spirit – to deal with lies and doubt that we wrestle with when we pray.

Even Satan himself will use Scripture, but in such a way that he twists and distorts the meaning so that it ceases to be God's truth, and becomes Satan's lies. This is precisely what the Devil did when he faced Jesus in the wilderness (Matt. 4.6–7).

(v) He is called 'the god of this world' (2 Cor. 4.4). He is 'the god of this age who has blinded the minds of unbelievers, so that they cannot see the light of the gospel of the glory of Christ, who is the image of God.' Woven into every work and plan of evangelism, whether a major campaign like Mission England, or one person sharing the gospel with a friend, is a spiritual struggle. Satan wants to keep people in darkness, Christ wants them to find Him as the Light of the world. Satan will attempt to keep people's eyes blind, but as we let the light of Jesus shine, and stand against Satan with believing prayer, we know that the darkness cannot overcome the light.

(vi) A roaring lion is how Peter described Satan in 1 Peter 5.8. If we were to meet a lion loose in the street we would almost certainly run away in fear. Fear is his stock method. Satan wants us to be afraid of death, of failure, of the future, of poverty, of suffering and many other things beside. When we are afraid Satan is usually at work, but 'Perfect love drives out fear' (1 John 4.18; cf. 2 Tim. 1.7). The truth is that if we resist Satan firm in our faith, then *he* is the one who flees!

The response of the Christian

Let me pause at this point and try to summarise what we have said so far. There is a war on with two kingdoms locked against each other – Christ versus Satan, the Spirit against the Flesh. Through His death and resurrection Christ has utterly defeated Satan and robbed him of his power. Satan, however, won't admit this and goes on fighting, pretending he can win, and he uses various tricks and ploys to attack the unsuspecting Christian. However, the believer is not only a child of God, he is a joint heir with Christ of this spiritual victory and in the hands of the individual Christian and of the church corporately lies practically the balance of power for blessing or defeat in the world.

Paul Bilheimer puts it thus:

> 'All the blessings of peace and tranquility, without which there can be no stable social order and no civilisation as we know it, are the results of the Gospel. . . . From the womb of the gospel are born all the principles, standards and qualities of character which form the foundation of all moral and spiritual, social and political well-being.'[2]

We have within our grasp the power of prayer as the decisive force and element to fashion the history of the world and to shape world events. We have to realise again 'that more things are wrought by prayer than this world dreams of'.

'To pray or not to pray?' – that is the question. And the answer will involve some very practical action!

The victory against Satan in practice

There are four instructions to share with you.

(i) Make sure you have your spiritual armour on! There is no point in going into the battle spiritually naked. Others have written fully about Paul's description of the armour in Ephesians 6.11–17; but let me remind you what God has given to us:

> 'Put on the full armour of God so that you can take your stand against the devil's schemes. For our struggle is not against flesh and blood but against the rulers, against the authorities, against the powers of this dark world and against the spiritual forces of evil in the heavenly realms. Therefore put on the full armour of God, so that when the day of evil comes, you may be able to stand your ground, and after you have done

everything, to stand. Stand firm then, with the belt of truth buckled round your waist, with the breastplate of righteousness in place, and with your feet fitted with the readiness that comes from the gospel of peace. In addition to all this, take up the shield of faith, with which you can extinguish all the flaming arrows of the evil one. Take the helmet of salvation and the sword of the Spirit, which is the word of God.'

We are called upon to put off or to renounce sinful habits and attitudes that will give Satan the opportunity to attack us. We are also called to take up, or to have put on already, the various pieces of God's armour.

We are to stand firm with the belt of truth around our waist – that truth which we have considered in the early part of the book. It is the truth that we are the children of God, that we have the authority of Jesus' name, and that we have the victory through our Saviour over Satan.

We have taken the breastplate of righteousness to confess to ourselves, to God and especially to Satan that though we are sinners by nature, we have been justified (regarded righteous by God) and wonderfully accepted by God through the shed blood of the Lord Jesus.

We are to have on the gospel sandals – our feet fitted with the readiness that comes from the gospel of peace. We are ready and willing to be used by the Lord. Rather like children dressed to go out for the day and standing at the front door, we are dressed to go out into the Lord's service, ready to meet whatever may come.

We have in our hands the shield of faith. Satan will fire at us, suddenly and without warning, the flaming darts of doubt, unbelief and temptation. We need to have our shield of faith available to deflect the attack and to put out the fires of the dart.

The helmet of salvation covers our heads and our minds. Whatever Satan may say, we take our stand upon the truth of God's saving word and the power of the name of Jesus.

Finally, in our other hand, we hold the sword of the Spirit – that particular word of God that we shall need in the moment of battle. We are ready for anything and everything.

Woe betide the Christian who fails to have on consciously the spiritual armour in the day of battle. With it, even against the spiritual forces ranged against us, we shall win.

(ii) Knowing we have the victory, resist Satan firm in your faith. You may want to memorise and claim such promises as these: 'You, dear children, are from God and have overcome them, because the one who is in you is greater than the one who is in the world,' and 'Everyone born of God overcomes the world. This is the victory that has overcome the world, even our faith' (1 John 4.4; 5.4).

Some years ago, I visited some mission hospitals in Kenya. One Saturday evening the matron, who was an Australian missionary, had invited a number of us, including the Head of the village, to her home for supper. During the course of the evening there was a thud at the door, and a man from the village who had drunk too much swayed before the house, intending to cause trouble for our hostess. Unfortunately, for him, he did not know that the Village Chief was present. When he came to the door in the matron's place, the drunken man fled away as quickly as his unsteady legs would carry him. What a picture of our Head man (Christ) dealing with Satan when he comes to trouble us!

(iii) Unfortunately for us, Satan won't give up easily, and we need to 'pray through' to an answer. This was the point of the story Jesus told about the widow who insisted on continually coming to the judge to win her case. As Luke puts it: 'Jesus told a parable to show them that they should always pray and not give up. . . . "However, when the Son of Man comes, will he find faith on the earth?" ' (Luke 18.1, 8). The faith that Jesus is looking for is not, in this case, a saving faith, but rather believing and persevering faith.

Paul Bilheimer puts it like this: 'God ordained prayer not primarily as a way of getting things done, but rather to enable the church as the Bride of Christ, to overcome Satan. . . . The Western Church has lost the prayer stamina of the mission church in Africa, Asia and South America, Indonesia and those of the underground church behind the Iron Curtain. We are great organisers, but poor pray-ers. Neglect of prayer is the one great reason for so few answers.'[2]

(iv) Lastly, but not least in importance, is the habit of Christians praying together. Jesus taught us of the power of two or three praying together:

> 'I tell you the truth, whatever you bind on earth will be bound in heaven, and whatever you loose on earth will be loosed in heaven. Again, I tell you that if two of you on earth agree about anything you ask for, it will be done for you by my Father in heaven. For where two or three come together in my name, there am I with them' (Matt. 18.18–20).

The early church knew this secret of the power of praying together – whether in praise, fellowship or in the battle against Satan. 'Together with one accord' and 'Together with one heart and mind' describes the church in Acts.

Jesus taught His disciples not only about the power of praying together, but of going out together two by two in their ministry for Him. We are to do the same when we wrestle in prayer against Satan. You may want to ask another Christian in the home or the fellowship to join you in prayer over a particular matter. If you are going out against spiritual forces or to face a known Satanic presence and influence then I believe you would be wrong to go alone, unless you have no other option – even so, tell other Christians about your ministry and get them to pray behind the scenes at home for you.

Rejoice in the victory and pray!

The needs may be great, the struggle may be hard and long, but what a privilege we have as the joint heirs with Christ. What power we have through His death and resurrection. What a weapon we have in prayer to win the victory over Satan. Let us use it faithfully.

Prayer and fasting

When the disciples failed to win the victory over the demons in the life of the epileptic boy, they came privately to Jesus to ask the reason for their defeat. Jesus told them: 'This kind can come out only by prayer and fasting' (Mark 9.29).

Fasting was an obligation upon the Jew in the Old Testament, but became a means of God's grace in the life of Christ and the early church (Matt. 4.2; 6.16; Acts 9.9; 13.2; 14.23; 1 Cor. 9.24–27; 2 Cor. 11.27 etc.)

Fasting is primarily the abstaining from food, or some other bodily activities, in order to seek the Lord more diligently. It may involve missing a meal, reducing the amount we eat, or, for those more experienced, fasting from between a day to a week or more. We fast to seek the Lord and His will, to humble ourselves before Him, to experience greater fellowship with Him and find power in His service.

Nowhere does the New Testament impose 'fasting' upon us, but many Christians are rediscovering it as a powerful means of God's grace. Charles H. Spurgeon recalled the days of fasting at the Metropolitan Tabernacle in London with pleasure: 'Our seasons of fasting and prayer have been highdays indeed. Never has Heaven's gate stood wider, never have our hearts been nearer the central glory.' Likewise, Charles Finney testified: 'Sometimes I would find myself empty of power. I would set aside a day for private prayer and fasting . . . after humbling myself and crying out for help, the power would return upon me with all its freshness.'[4]

Fasting is not essential to victory over Satan, but it may well be the missing means of grace that more Christians and churches need to discover for themselves.

Chapter Seven: Notes

1. Paul Bilheimer, *Destined for the Throne* (Kingsway, Eastbourne, 1975) p. 18.
2. ibid., pp. 60 and 61.
3. ibid., pp. 15 and 101.
4. Arthur Wallis, *God's Chosen Fast* (Victory Press, 1968) is very helpful in teaching fully about fasting.

Eight: Praise – The Missing Element

My wife and I have known Pam for more than twenty-five years. As well as being a nursing sister at the Leeds General Infirmary, and then at Scarborough Hospital, she was the bridesmaid at our wedding. She then responded to the Lord's call to serve him in Pakistan with the Church Missionary Society at Quetta and Bannu Hospitals. While out in Pakistan, she met and married Raj, and now with their three growing children, they live in a fairly remote part of that country. We have been 'phoning them fairly regularly recently because Raj was ill, and they had come to Karachi for hospital treatment where he faced the possibility of having his foot amputated. As individuals and as a church, we kept up that regular 'phone link for a few months to get the latest news and to support and encourage Pam. On occasions she had time to write to us. In one of her letters she wrote:

> 'I still get assailed with doubt – I thought I was not doubting, however, it came out in my dreams the night before, so I cannot afford to be complacent, and I have to take active measures myself to keep on thanking and praising, expecting and visualising the healing.'

Praise God that healing is now taking place, and Pam and Raj are looking forward to being back home with their children and work and villagers, but in the midst of the battle and the months of watching and waiting Pam had to keep on praising.

Praise was once, seemingly, the missing element in the church's life. Very little had been written about it in the spiritual classics on prayer. Now we face the problem of calling every new hymn- or song-book '. . . . Praise'. Pity the latest hymn book that doesn't have 'Praise' in its title! From being the missing element, praise is now in danger of becoming the overworked emphasis. If we would praise God aright we must understand what praise is, why we are to praise Him, what are the blessings of praise, and what it will mean in our personal prayer life.

What is praise?

Three different words are used in the Old Testament for 'Praise'.

(i) *Halal* This has the basic idea of making a noise, but it can also involve movement, and it helps us to see that praise is not just expressed with our lips, but may involve the lifting of our hands, and moving our bodies so that 'All that is within me can bless His holy name' (Ps. 103.1, RSV).

(ii) *Zamar* means what it sounds – the playing of an instrument or the making of music. Psalm 150 – just to mention one Psalm – calls us to praise God for His acts of power and for His surpassing greatness. How are we to do this? With the trumpet, the harp and lyre, the tambourine and dancing, the strings and flute, with the clash of the cymbals and the resounding cymbals. (Two kinds of cymbals – small and large – were involved.) The Jewish hymn book, the Psalter, ends with Psalm 150 verse 6: 'Let everything that has breath praise the LORD. Praise the LORD!' A glorious Hallelujah concludes the book.

(iii) *Yada* is the third word and it means to know intimately, and consequently to appreciate and praise someone. It is the same word used to describe the personal and intimate relationship between a husband and wife. I don't talk *about* the Lord, I talk *to* the Lord. I don't talk about worship, I worship the Lord personally and freely. Among the various 'helps' I have in my personal devotional life is a copy of *Mission Praise*, the collection of old and new hymns and songs originally published for Mission England. I often find myself turning to Number 279:

You are the King of Glory,
You are the Prince of Peace,
You are the Lord of heav'n and earth,
You're the Son of righteousness.
Angels bow down before You,
Worship and adore,
For You have the words of eternal life,
You are Jesus Christ the Lord.
Hosanna to the Son of David!
Hosanna to the King of kings!
Glory in the highest heaven
for Jesus the Messiah reigns![1]

Such words help me to express my praise and worship to the Lord and love Him.

Praise and thanksgiving

Praise is acknowledging *who God is*. Thanksgiving is recognising *what God has done*. Praise concerns His *character*, whilst thanksgiving concerns His *conduct*. They are different, but both will lead into adoration and worship. Take Psalm 95. Praise and thanksgiving are linked together and as the worship proceeds, the worshipper's mood and expression change and develop. In verses 1 and 2 the people enter the temple with joy, they shout aloud, they come before the Lord with thanksgiving, they extol His name with music and song. Then they begin to reflect and meditate more about the nature of the Lord in verses 3 and 5. The Lord is a great God, He is above all gods. The deep places of the earth are in His hand, and the very mountain tops belong to Him. He made the sea and the dry land. No wonder that the mood changes! The exuberant joy and praise have become the deeper reverence and hushed adoration in verses 6 and 7. 'Come, let us bow down in worship, let us kneel before the LORD our Maker;' you almost sense the silence in the crowded Temple as the naturally outgoing and demonstrative crowd are hushed in awe and majestic reverence before the Lord. They are knowing Him. They are expressing their relationship with Him, and their worship continues as they acknowledge that 'He is our God, and we are the people of His pasture, and the flock under His care.'

Just as a married couple need to go on learning to love and to express their love to each other in ever deeper ways, so the Christian and the Church need to grow in worshipping the Lord. Just as it is a dangerous sign when a marriage becomes dull and formal, so it can be with our worship and praise and thanksgiving.

On earth praise is the thermometer of the believer's spiritual life, and in heaven it is the constant activity of the angels and the elders around the throne. In the Bible, praise is the thread that runs right the way through. Moses (Exod. 15) and Deborah the prophetess (Judg. 5) both praise God for His deliverance. Hannah praises God for the gift of a son, Samuel (1 Sam. 2) and amongst all the contrasting human moods and conditions of the soul – from despair and depression to delight and dancing – will be found a group of Psalms full of praise (Pss. 104–106, 111–118 and 146–150.) The New Testament also contains many songs of glory to the Lord (called doxologies – from two Greek words meaning 'uttering praise') and there are the glorious passages of worship recorded for us in Revelation. (See, for example, Rom. 11.33–36; 16.25–27; Eph. 3.20–21; Jude 24; Rev. 5; 7).

Why praise God?

Just as there are times when our hearts overflow with praise and adoration and love to the Lord, so there are also times when we find our hearts cold and dull and unresponsive to the Lord. Praise, however, does not just involve the emotions, but also the mind and the will. If, therefore, we only praise God when we feel like it, we have not learnt the reasons and ways of praising Him at all times.

'We praise him, not because we feel like it, nor necessarily because we have remembered some of the marvellous things that He has done for us, but simply because He is the Lord and therefore always worthy of our praise.'[2]

While that is true, the Scriptures are also full of reasons why we should praise Him. Let me give you some of the reasons:

(i) Because of everything that God has made in creation (Pss. 104; 150).

(ii) Because of the name – or character – of the Lord. 'Not to us, O LORD, not to us but to your name be the glory, because of Your love and faithfulness' (Ps. 115.1).

(iii) Because God has given us His Word. 'In God, whose word I praise, in the LORD, whose word I praise – In God I trust; I will not be afraid' (Ps. 56.10–11).

(iv) Because the Lord Jesus has come into the world and reveals God to us personally (Luke 2.13–14).

(v) Because of every spiritual blessing that we have in Christ. 'Praise be to the God and Father of our Lord Jesus Christ, who has blessed us in the heavenly realms with every spiritual blessing in Christ' (Eph. 1.3).

As well as the unchanging reasons for praise, every believer will have his own reasons for praise – the answers to prayer, the protection in travel, the provision of a need, and we sense that we can never exhaust the list of why we should and can praise the Lord.

The results of praise

If the reasons for praise are many, so are the results, but I want to focus on five particular blessings that can come to every Christian's life.

(i) *Praise magnifies the Lord* When Mary had heard the message of the angel Gabriel that she was to be the mother of the Lord Jesus she burst into praise. 'My soul does magnify the Lord, and my spirit rejoices in God my Saviour' (Luke 1.46, RSV).

Mary's praise didn't make God any bigger, but it did enlarge her own vision and understanding of God.

For many years now I have collected New Zealand stamps – as and when I can. From time to time I need to use a magnifying glass to see something on the stamp more clearly. In doing so, I don't make the stamp or any part of the stamp larger, but I see that part more clearly. As we praise God so we make our awareness of Him greater, and we are the more ready to give Him His rightful place at the beginning of the day. For example, we can either get out of bed feeling fed up with the monotony that lies ahead of us at the office or in the home, or we can praise and say 'This is the day the Lord has made, we will rejoice and be glad in it'. The Lord doesn't change, but our attitude to the day and everyone we meet throughout the day will be changed. As we praise God we declare His sovereignty over the day and we also put the pressures and the demands of the world into proper perspective.

When we praise God our life becomes God-centred rather than man-centred. It would appear that God has a strange economic order. He has told us to seek first His kingdom and righteousness and then all other things – food and clothes etc. – will be ours as well. We are so often tempted to stagger through the day under our own steam with the intention of praising and praying when we get time. Whereas God says that if we put Him into the centre of the day and begin with praise and prayer, we shall find that we have time for everything that needs to be done, and often a little more as well. Martin Luther once said: 'I have so many things to do today that I must spend three or four hours in prayer to start with.'

By contrast many will feel they have so little time for prayer and praise. Archbishop William Temple was once asked how he would spend three minutes if that was all the time he had available for prayer. His answer was: 'I would spend two minutes and thirty seconds in praise, and thirty seconds in petition.' I wonder what answer we would have given. We move too readily into asking before we have really praised the Lord. That is true of our personal prayer life and our church prayer meetings. Prayer is incomplete without praise as life is incomplete without breathing.

(ii) *Praise edifies the Christian* Have you discovered Isaiah 61.3 in your Bible? It says that God will give to His people 'The oil of gladness instead of mourning, and a garment of praise instead of a spirit of despair. They will be called oaks of righteousness, a planting of the Lord for the display of His splendour.'

Pam, out in Karachi, had spoken of despair in her letter but she also added: 'The lifting up of the hands (Heb. 12.12) is a reminder to me to keep praising when I am excessively weary.' There will be many Christians who will know weariness for one reason or another and the Lord longs that they should praise Him. Praise will build us up, strengthen and encourage us. Satan longs to weaken us and break us up through fear, guilt or worry, but the Lord wants to plant us as strong oaks that do not yield to the cold winds of temptation and testing.

Paul Bilheimer reminds us: 'The missing element of faith that does not triumph is praise – perpetual, purposeful, aggressive praise. Praise is the highest form of prayer because it combines petition with faith. The secret of answered prayer is faith without doubt. And the secret of faith without doubt is praise'.[3]

Tom Smail testifies to the difference praise made when praying for Northern Ireland. 'In our praying amidst the Northern Ireland troubles we learned that to begin with intercession is to end with depression, but to begin with praise is to come to the point where we can ask in hope!'[4]

(iii) *Praise promotes holy living* In his letter, James makes this penetrating statement: 'With the tongue we praise our Lord and Father, and with it we curse men, who have been made in God's likeness. Out of the same mouth come praise and cursing. My brothers, this should not be' (Jas. 3.9–10). When something goes wrong at work, or at home or within the Christian fellowship, sadly and too often we find that Christians will blame someone else, will jump to the wrong conclusions or even curse a brother or a sister. As James so simply puts it – 'my brothers this should not be.' Praise will cause us to cleanse and purify our hearts and our lips and promote holiness, for we know that if we are to offer acceptable praise to God, we must have 'clean hands and a pure heart' with men.

(iv) *Praise makes our evangelism effective* (It has an effect upon the world, and upon Satan.) Often the most effective forms of evangelism we have known in our church life have been linked with times of praise. As we have praised God during a communion service, He has become so real that men have turned to Him. I think of one married couple in the fellowship who constantly seek to keep Jesus at the centre of their living and loving. They seek to give praise to the Lord in all circumstances, and I am not surprised to hear the stories of other people who through their ministry have come to faith in Jesus or been helped on in their Christian lives. They have seen the reality of Jesus in the lives of others.

It was just like this in the Acts of the Apostles. As Paul and Silas, his travelling companion, praised God in the darkness of a Philippian jail at midnight, having been wrongfully arrested and imprisoned, it was not surprising that the other prisoners took notice. Even stranger was the fact that when the prisoners could have escaped, following the earthquake, they remained where they were. The jailer, fearing for his own life if any prisoners escaped, could only come trembling before Paul to ask what he had to do to be saved. 'Believe in the Lord Jesus, and you will be saved – you and your household,' was Paul's answer (Acts 16.31).

The same was true on the Day of Pentecost. The Twelve first of all praised the Lord, and then Peter stood up and preached the good news of Jesus – crucified and risen from the dead.

We need not only the truth of the gospel to convince our minds, but also the praises of the gospel to open our hearts and lives to the Saviour himself.

(v) *Praise defeats Satan* 'I say the doxology and dismiss the devil' said a Christian worker once. We are told to resist the devil and he will flee from us. The best way to resist him is to affirm our faith in God. As a result we grow strong in our faith, and Satan flees. In the Old Testament when Jehoshaphat faced certain defeat at the hands of Moab and Ammon (2 Chr. 20) he did not know what to do, but his eyes were steadfastly fixed on God. God told him not to be afraid or discouraged because of the vast army.

> ' "For the battle is not yours, but God's. . . . Do not be afraid; do not be discouraged. Go out to face them tomorrow, and the Lord will be with you." . . . Jehoshaphat appointed men to sing to the LORD and to praise Him for the splendour of His holiness as they went out at the head of the army, saying: "Give thanks to the Lord, for His love endures forever." As they began to sing and praise, the LORD set ambushes against the men of Ammon and Moab' (2 Chr. 20.15–23).

Judah means praise, and Judah was to go ahead of the

army with praise. On this occasion praise was very clearly a part of God's plan to defeat the enemy. Likewise, praise is part of God's plan for us to defeat Satan. It is said of Corrie Ten Boom, in her solitary confinement in prison, that she began each day by singing – 'Stand up, Stand up for Jesus'. By exalting the Saviour, she defeated Satan.

Praise in daily life

Each of us will have our own way of praising the Lord, but some practical guidelines may help and encourage you.

(i) *Praise God spontaneously* We were just dropping off to sleep one night at about 11.30 p.m. when one of the children walked into our bedroom to say they had missed being killed by a car travelling very fast on the main road by about five inches. On some other occasion my instinctive reaction might well have been to give them a lesson in crossing roads, but on this occasion it was a very definite 'Praise the Lord'. It doesn't matter where you are – out shopping, at a difficult interview, coping with a hectic day – you can quite naturally, quietly or loudly (depending on your personality and surroundings), follow the Psalmist's command to 'Praise the Lord'.

(ii) *Praise the Lord sacrificially* Hebrews 13.15–16 says: 'Through Jesus, therefore, let us continually offer to God a sacrifice of praise – the fruit of lips that confess His name. And do not forget to do good and to share with others, for with such sacrifices God is pleased.' At times, praise may be difficult. It may seem more like a sacrifice, and demand considerable determination, consciously and deliberately, to praise God, but it will be rewarding. We do not just think 'praise'; we are to speak it out, and bless others as well as God. To some Christians this may not come easily or naturally, so we need to learn to praise God and work at it.

(iii) *Praise the Lord in the Spirit* Paul, in Ephesians 5.18–20, writes, 'Be filled with the Spirit. Speak to one another with psalms, hymns and spiritual songs. Sing and make music in your hearts to the Lord, always giving thanks to God the Father for everything, in the name of the Lord Jesus Christ.'

There is a clear link between knowing the fulness of the Spirit and praising the Lord. As we allow the Spirit to fill us, so praise will flow out to the Lord. As praise flows out, so we shall know more of the Holy Spirit going on filling us and making Jesus more and more wonderful to us. 'It is only by the power of the Spirit that people worship God as He really is. That is why all the revivals in the history of the church have been accompanied by great singing and praise.'[5] One particular way in which we praise God in the Spirit is by using the gift of tongues. Tongues is a gift available to all believers, and known by many. Some Christians find that God gives them a tongue when they do not know what to pray. Others find that *over*-flowing praise is expressed in tongues when human words are inadequate to communicate their praise and worship and love to the Lord. I like to think of tongues at such a time as going into 'automatic gear' in praise. Many have testified to the fact of special times of praise going on for quite a time – it may be half an hour, it may be much longer. We have been lifted up out of ourselves into the very presence of God and as the hymn puts it been 'lost in wonder, love and praise'.

In her dramatic and remarkable story of effective Christian witness within the walled city of Hong Kong, *Chasing the Dragon*, Jackie Pullinger gives an eloquent testimony to the value of praising God in the Spirit. Tongues to her were not only a means of praise, but an avenue of power against Satan, and a channel of God's effective working within the lives of men and women bound by drugs and gripped by the fear of the Triad Gangs. More and more Christians are discovering that God gives a freedom in praying in the Spirit to very young Christians in a remarkable way, not only in these exceptional circumstances in Hong Kong, but in routine and ordinary lives elsewhere.

(iv) *Praise the Lord specifically* 'Count your blessings, name them one by one, and it will surprise you what the Lord has done.' It is when we take time to list in detail all that the Lord has done for us that we realise the greatness of His mercy, and the goodness of His grace. The grumbling spirit will give way to the grateful heart when we stop and remember all the way the Lord has led us.

When the Psalmist faced the question 'How can I repay the LORD for all His goodness to me?' he gave the answer 'I will lift up the cup of salvation and call on the name of the LORD. I will fulfil my vows to the LORD in the presence of all His people' (Ps. 116.12–14). C. S. Lewis made the same point as he pondered on the wonder of human happiness. 'I had never noticed that all enjoyment spontaneously overflows into praise.[6]

(v) *Praise the Lord with singing* There are more than three hundred different commands in the Bible to sing to the Lord, or to praise the name of the Lord with singing. Singing has been a significant feature of the revivals of the church; it is a secret weapon we have against Satan's attack; it makes use of the ready-made songs and hymns of the Christian Church to express our love and devotion to the Lord, and the act of singing helps to set free our inner emotions that our culture has often forced us to lock away. We may not think we have a very tuneful voice, but it is with our soul that we are to sing to the Lord: 'My heart is steadfast, O God; I will sing and make music with all my soul' (Psalm 108.1). 'There is no aspect of worship so powerful and yet so neglected as the aspect of singing in personal prayer'.[7]

As we are continually aware of the Lord's goodness and blessing, whether we are enjoying flowers, or a football match, or a person, so we shall continually praise Him. Praise will turn living from an existence to be endured to a delight to be enjoyed. As the Psalmist said (34.1): 'I will extol the LORD at all times; his praise shall always be on my lips.' At least for one believer praise was not the missing element.

Chapter Eight: Notes

1. 'You are the King of Glory' by Mavis Ford © 1978, Springtide/Word Music (UK), (A Division of Word (UK) Ltd), Northbridge Road, Berkhamsted, Herts. HP4 1EH. England. Used by permission.
2. David Watson, *I Believe in Evangelism* (Hodder and Stoughton, 1976) p. 159.
3. Paul Bilheimer, *Destined for the Throne* (Kingsway, Eastbourne, 1975) p. 18.
4. Tom Smail, *The Forgotten Father* (Hodder & Stoughton, 1980) p. 164.
5. David Watson, *Discipleship* (Hodder & Stoughton, 1981) p. 105.
6. C. S. Lewis, *Reflections on the Psalms* (Fontana Books, 1962) p. 80.
7. Judson Cornwall, *Let us Praise* (Logos International, 1973) pp. 82–84.

Nine: Confession is Good for the Soul

There are praise meetings, prayer meetings, meetings to intercede – for special areas of the world, pressing problems or personal crises. There may be times when we quite deliberately wait upon the Lord to know His guidance, but after more than twenty-five years in the Christian ministry I cannot recall hearing about – let alone attending – a meeting specifically promoted to help God's people confess their sin and their need! I want to focus on 'confession' and plead for a recovery of confession in our Christian lives.

What is confession?

The word itself means to acknowledge, admit or agree. It can relate to the Lord or to us. It can describe something positive or negative. Daniel is an outstanding example of confession in the Old Testament.

In Daniel chapter 9 we read: 'So I turned to the Lord God and pleaded with Him in prayer and petition, in fasting, and in sackcloth and ashes. I prayed to the LORD my God and confessed: "O Lord, the great and awesome God, who keeps His covenant of love with all who love Him and obey His commands, we have sinned and done wrong. We have been wicked and have rebelled; we have turned away from your commands and laws" ' (Dan. 9.3–5).

In those words Daniel related confession positively to the Lord and negatively to himself, earthing his prayer in the conditions in which he and the captive people of

God found themselves at the beginning of the reign of Darius, the King in Babylon.

It is possible therefore to liken 'confession' to an electric plug. If it is going to work it must have both negative and positive points and be well earthed.

Confession involves the acknowledgement and the profession of our faith. It is linked with an admission of failure. It is not easy to confess our disobedience and shortcomings, but it produces some marvellously healthy fruit and blessings.

Confession and faith

Confession must include the positive affirmation of what we believe and whom we trust.

For the apostle Peter, the turning points in his Christian experience came, not only when he confessed 'Go away from me, Lord, I am a sinful man!' but also when he confessed 'You are the Christ, the Son of the Living God' (see Luke 5.8; Matt. 16.16).

'I am . . .' – 'You are . . .' – both are confessions. The first event happened after the experienced fishermen had spent a night fishing without any success. Then Jesus, the carpenter, came and taught these men their trade. Jesus had been teaching the people from Peter's borrowed boat, at the edge of the lake. Then he asked the fishermen to row out further into the deep, and told them to let their nets down over the side of the boat. They caught such a large number of fish that their nets began to break. With the help of their partners in the other boat they hauled the catch of fish on land.

Peter had sat at the oars and heard the message of Jesus. He toiled at the nets and saw the miracle of Jesus, and all he was able to do in response was to fall at Jesus' feet and confess his own unworthiness and sinfulness, urging the Master to leave. As Peter admitted to Jesus his weakness, frustration, failure and sinfulness, so Jesus revealed more and more and more of His power and purposes to him. As we confess our sin and need, so we receive more of Jesus.

It is also Peter who reminds us of the other side of confession: 'You are . . .'. Contrary to popular opinion, local gossip and misunderstanding, Jesus was not John the Baptist, or Elijah, or another prophet. He was the Christ, the Son of God. It was a confession that now made it possible for Jesus to teach his friends something more about his purposes, that He had come to suffer, to die and to save men.

Just as the negative confession about himself, 'I am not . . .', led Peter to discipleship, so the positive confession 'You are the Christ' led those same disciples to a new experience of understanding God's purposes.

Confession – whether negative or positive – will be creative. Consider Paul's words in Romans 10.9–10: 'If you confess with your mouth, "Jesus is Lord", and believe in your heart that God raised him from the dead, you will be saved. For it is with the heart that you believe and are justified, and it is with your mouth that you confess and are saved.'

If we only 'think' our faith in our hearts we come into a new relationship with God – we are regarded just as if we have never sinned (justified), but if we also speak the word out loud, and confess with our lips, then we know, and find assurance thereby, that we are saved. There is a creative work done when words are spoken.

It was so in the beginning: 'God said . . . and it was so' (Gen. 1.11, 14 etc.)

Both rightful thinking and audible confession have a part to play in effective prayer. 'If any individual does not believe in his heart the confession his lips are making, then it will not work. The confession of Satan's ability to hinder and to keep from success gives Satan dominion over the individual.'[1]

Immediately after Peter had confessed that Jesus was the Christ he stumbled, and rejected what Jesus had just said about His own death and resurrection: 'Never Lord, this shall never happen to you!' Jesus turned and said to

Peter, 'Out of my sight, Satan! You are a stumbling block to me; you do not have in mind the things of God, but the things of men' (Matt. 16.22–23).

Jesus did not think his confession against Satan, he spoke it out. Such confession puts Satan to flight; it also stimulates and edifies the faith of the believer.

Why is this? What are we actually doing when we verbally confess our faith in prayer. Firstly, we are making statements about who God, or who Jesus, is. God protects, cares, forgives, guides, Jesus saves, loves etc. As we 'speak out' and personally confess (during a time of prayer) some aspect of God's character, so faith will rise and prayer will be strengthened.

Secondly, we are affirming quite clearly the promises and the truths of God's word. We affirm the truth of God's word to ourselves, to our fears, to Satan, and to God himself. We activate the promise, and faith again rises.

Thirdly, we are working out the spiritual process Paul writes about in Romans 10. 'Faith comes from hearing the message, and the message is heard through the word of Christ' (17).

The promises of God, on which our faith rests, and which give life to our prayers, are linked with different parts of our human bodies. Our eyes see the promises on the printed page, our mouth can speak them out, our ears hear the same word, our hearts begin to grasp their truth, our mind takes hold of it, and our faith expands, and we begin to trust God for more and more. When we confess the truth of God's word we are affirming the grace and ability of God. 'We must understand that God moves in line with His word. We shall treat His word with the same reverence we would treat Jesus, as if He were here in the flesh.'[2]

So we see the part that the Scriptures play in prayer. They are like a mirror that reflects ourselves, but they are also a mirror that reflects and reveals God. They may show our unworthiness, but they also display His worthiness. They may show how often we have broken our promises but they also reveal all the promises that God himself will keep without fail.

Let me share an example of the value of speaking out in prayer. It was just before Christmas, and about twenty church members were meeting to pray for the Lord's blessing upon the whole range of Christmas services – carols round the tree, Communion services, as well as the main Family Services. We were praying in a rather generally-not-expecting very much to happen kind of way, until someone present shared with us that before the prayer meeting, earlier in the day, they had asked the Lord how many people He was clearly wanting to bless. Was it 60, 50, 40, 30, etc? – (a little like Abraham and Sodom in reverse – see Genesis 18). It seemed as if the Lord was saying He wanted specifically to bless 40 people. We took that figure as being from the Lord, knowing that the word of knowledge would not have been easily gained or lightly shared. Suddenly the prayer meeting moved up at least a couple of gears in expectancy, in specific praying and in the number of people leading in prayer. A rather mundane time of prayer suddenly became alive. God had given us a very special promise. How do you know when God has fulfilled His promise? How do you know He has met with 40 people? In the light of the word of knowledge, it seemed sensible to make each service evangelistic, and to offer people an evangelistic booklet afterwards if they had responded to the preaching of the gospel. This we did after each service, and after each service people responded. By the time I had said farewell to the congregation after the main service, I knew that 37 booklets had been given out. I went to my colleague to ask how many he had given out. Three! But there was still one more service to go, and after every other service (and there had been five already) people had responded. At the last service no one outwardly responded. One of the best moments of Christmas was to go home and report that God had given us exactly 40 people. There was no way it could have been organised, except by Him.

Specific promises given by God lead to definite prayers offered to God in faith, and heart-felt praise arising to Him. He gets the glory, and we find our faith stronger. We will need to confess in our prayers what we have not done. We will also need to confess what Jesus has done and has promised to us in prayer. 'I am a sinful man. . . .' 'You are the Christ, the Son of the living God.'

Confession and failure

'There will never come a time when we don't need to confess.'[3] So wrote Dr Graham Scroggie. Such is the need of the human heart that until we arrive in glory and are made perfect, we shall need to admit our failure and sin to the Lord.

Such confession will admit what we have done, and what we have failed to do. It can't be put much better than in the words from the Book of Common Prayer. 'We have followed too much the devices and desires of our own hearts. We have offended against thy holy laws. We have left undone those things which we ought to have done, and we have done those things which we ought not to have done.'[4]

The 1980 Alternative Prayer Book states: 'Almighty God, our Heavenly Father, we have sinned against you, and against our fellow men, in thought and word and deed, through negligence, through weakness, through our own deliberate fault.'

The Psalmist puts it this way: 'Who can discern his errors? Forgive my hidden faults. Keep your servant also from wilful sins; may they not rule over me. Then will I be blameless, innocent of great transgression' (Ps. 19.12–13). There he describes his errors, hidden faults, wilful sins and transgression.

So we are reminded not only of the need to admit and confess that we are sinners by nature, and therefore sinners in action, but also that we are sinners in general and sinners in very specific details. It is healthy and helpful to confess the details of our sin and disobedience in prayer to God – whether it be that we have lost our temper, spoken hastily about someone, been dishonest, been unfair at home, or not owned up to something wrong we have done. If we confess a particular sin, then we shall have the blessing and peace of that particular sin being forgiven.

This doesn't mean that we are to be unhealthily introspective, looking deeply into our lives and raking up the muck of the past that God has *already* dealt with. But where God shows us there is unconfessed sin, we are to confess that sin to Him and know and receive His forgiveness. Once we have received forgiveness, we know that God will remember our sin no more, and we are to do the same both to our sins and the sins of other people.

I never tire of reading those reassuring promises of John's first letter: 'If we confess our sins, He is faithful and just and will forgive us our sins and purify us from all unrighteousness' (1 John 1.9).

If we confess our failure in our prayers, we shall never need to go to God and say 'I've done it again.' God will say to us. 'Done what again? I have no record of what you have done.' God has cast all our sins into the depths of the sea, and, as Corrie Ten Boom has said, God has set up a notice by them saying 'No fishing'. God has cast all our sin behind His back – where He can't see them. He has removed our transgressions from us as far as the East is from the West (Ps. 103.12). While you can measure the distance between the North and the South Poles, you cannot measure East to West!

It is to God that we first and foremost confess our sin and failure, and it is He alone who will forgive and wipe the record clear. We do not therefore need to engage in 'auricular confession to a priest' as a spiritual requirement before we can receive the forgiveness of sin. No priest forgives, but God alone.

There may well be times, however, when we need to confess our sin and rebellion to others who have been affected by what we have done. We may need to have the assurance of their forgiveness, and the reconciliation of our own relationship with them. We may find that the burden of sin at special times is so great that it is helpful to us personally to share the situation with another older and more mature Christian, to seek their counsel and to know the assurance of forgiveness. It is sometimes a help not only to 'think' our confession but to speak it out loud.

The Prodigal Son did just that. While he was in the far country looking after the pigs he worked out in his mind exactly what he would say to his father. He had thought out his plan of confession, but when he came back to his father he needed to speak it out. Before he had time to finish, however, he knew the love and forgiveness of his father. He knew all was forgiven and the past dealt with. For him – and for millions of Christians – true confession will bring lasting blessings.

Some prayers of confession

In addition to the Prodigal Son's prayer of confession, we have the experience of Isaiah (Isa. 6); of King David (2 Sam. 11–12; Ps. 51); of Nehemiah (Neh. 1); and of Daniel (Dan. 9.)

All were great men – Prophet, King, Leader and Prime Minister in exile, yet all had to come to the place of confession of their own sin, and the sins of the people they were leading. Isaiah had to confess that the very parts of his body – his lips and mouth – that were used so much in the service of God were unclean, and needed to be purified and dedicated afresh to the service of God. King David, great as he was, and though known as the sweet Psalmist of Israel and the man after God's own heart, had to confess the depth of his sin and degradation in his personal relationships.

For different reasons, both Nehemiah and Daniel had to identify with the sin of God's people and come to Him in confession. Nehemiah led the return to Jerusalem of the remnant of God's people and began to rebuild the city and its walls. First of all, however, he had to come to God in humility, repentance and confession (Nehemiah 1). In a similar way, but while the people were still in captivity in Babylon, Daniel identified with his peoples' sin. His most remarkable prayer is recorded for us in Daniel chapter 9 . . . The whole prayer takes up sixteen verses. Only in the last three verses does Daniel ask anything of the Lord, and that is only to hear, to have mercy, to act and to forgive for the sake of the Lord's name. The other thirteen verses are taken up with the greatness, mercy, compassion, majesty and character of the Lord, or with the disobedience, rebellion and sin of his people and of Daniel himself. Yet Daniel was the man who sought to obey God in every situation, the man who continued to pray three times a day even though he knew he would be thrown to the lions in punishment.

There are other great prayers of confession among the treasures of the Church. The prayers of Archbishop Lancelot Andrewes are one example. Andrewes was appointed a Canon of St Paul's Cathedral and revived the old custom of walking up and down the aisles of the Cathedral at stated times in case any visitors wished to come to him for spiritual help. In 1601 Andrewes became Dean of Westminster at a time when King James authorised a new translation of the Bible – which we know, and many treasure, as the Authorised Version. (Andrewes himself helped with the translation of Genesis to 1 Chronicles.) Shortly afterwards he became the Bishop of Chichester, and then Bishop of Winchester.

It was said of him that as a lecturer or teacher he was 'Doctor Andrewes', and in the pulpit he was 'Bishop Andrewes', but in his own room at private prayer, he was 'Saint Andrewes'. He would spend about five hours each day at his prayers, and, while he used some Christian and Jewish service books when he prayed, he depended first and foremost on the Bible. For him it was impossible to improve on what the Scriptures said.

His published book of prayers is divided into sections on thanksgiving, praise, intercession and confession.

His prayers of confession reflect those marvellous prayers of confession in the Old Testament. We would do well to read them, and begin to make some of their truths and phrases our own.[5]

The blessings of confession

I wonder if you have ever discovered the many blessings we are promised when we confess our sin.

(i) As sin is confessed, so the sinner's life is cleansed (1 John 1.9). Just as people's homes need to be cleaned up after the sea has swept over and broken down the sea-wall defences, so the surge of sinfulness and lawlessness in the world breaks the banks and overruns the boundaries of God's law and comes swirling into our lives. As wickedness increases – with the misuse of sex and drugs, and the occult, with dishonesty, cheating and the wholesale breakdown of law and order – so we may well personally feel the need for more frequent confession and cleansing. Praise God that the blood of the Lord Jesus Christ goes on cleansing us from all sin (1 John 1.7).

(ii) We shall find mercy in confession – and in return begin to show mercy to others. 'He who conceals his sins does not prosper, but whosoever confesses and renounces them finds mercy' (Prov. 28.13). The end of the twentieth century is becoming an increasingly violent age. Why are men and women harsh and brutal to one another? Why do nations want to hurt one another, and neighbour strike against neighbour? Sin has hardened their hearts and souls. If they had confessed their rebellion and violence against God they would have prospered, they would have found mercy from others, and shown mercy. We all know the experience of someone saying to us: 'If they'll say sorry, then I'll say sorry.' But the

Bible teaches us that if we show mercy we shall receive mercy. If we admit need, we shall find that need met.

(iii) Sometimes unconfessed sin affects our bodily and mental health, so that when we eventually admit our sin we find that our physical or mental needs are also met. So long as David refused to confess his adultery with Bathsheba, and his murder of Uriah, he wasted away bodily. His testimony is that when he got right spiritually, he began to get right physically.

'Blessed is he whose transgressions are forgiven, whose sins are covered. . . . When I kept silent, my bones wasted away through my groaning all day long. For day and night your hand was heavy upon me, my strength was sapped as in the heat of summer. Then I acknowledged my sin to you, and did not cover up my iniquity. I said, "I will confess my transgressions to the LORD" – and you forgave the guilt of my sin' (Ps. 32.1–5).

The same connection between wholeness of our personality, on the one hand, and the confession of sin, on the other, is also made in James' passage about praying for the sick.

'The prayer offered in faith will make the sick person well; the Lord will raise him up. If he has sinned, he will be forgiven. Therefore confess your sins to each other, and pray for each other so that you may be healed' (Jas. 5.15–16).

Isn't it true to our experience that a clear conscience and a quiet spirit and soul will lead to a healthier body and a healthier mind? There is something wholesome and life-giving that comes to us personally when we confess our need, our sin and our failure to the Lord.

(iv) Confession will lead to a healing of relationships with others. Our attitudes to and relationships with other people will be changed, and the effectiveness of our witness and living as Christians will have a new power and reality.

A personal testimony

The benefits and blessings of confession are real but, as I can testify, we are often slow to respond to God's promptings.

It has been my habit, when free on a Saturday evening, to go into church and pray for the Lord's blessing on the worship and preaching of the next day. I would walk round the church praying for members of the congregation. I would seek the Lord's blessing and help for the ministry. Because I knew I was humanly alone, I was able to open my heart to the Lord.

One Saturday, when I was about to leave after prayer, I was aware that Jesus Himself stood at one of the side doors of the church, near the choir stalls. He moved slowly into the chancel, and I fell before Him. He evoked from me a mixture of awe, wonder and thrill. Then I heard His voice: 'Michael, may I come into the midst of my church?' What a question! It was His church! It is His church! Why was He asking? Wasn't He already in control? What was taking the central place in our church, which was rightly His? The questions rushed into my mind, and I was anxious to show the Lord that He could. I wanted to take Him round the church and introduce Him to various people, but then He disappeared, but the question remained. 'Michael, may I come into the midst of my church?' (Rev. 3.20).

We were due out to dinner with friends that evening and I dared not say anything to anyone about what had happened. The next morning I happened to be preaching on the theme of 'Is Jesus the Son of God?' It seemed fitting to end the sermon with the story of what had happened the night before. I know of at least one church member whose faith was restored by that experience.

From then on, God kept nudging and speaking to us as a church. Again and again over the next few years we were reminded that we were like the church at Laodicea. We may have had a reputation in the area with men, but as God looked at us He had to tell us we were self-sufficient and proud, and like the Laodiceans protesting that we needed nothing, not realising that we were wretched, pitiful, poor, blind and naked. We had to repent – oh, the times that word and command came to us as a church – and then we had to invite Jesus to come into the midst of the church (the true exposition of Rev. 3.20)!

It was not until early 1985, during a week of prayer, that the church at last repented. We were gathered in prayer in church on the Wednesday of that week and the Holy Spirit brought us corporately to that point where we knew we had to and wanted to repent. Until we did so, there was no point in trying to do anything else. The church asked me to lead us all in an act of repentance. After a period of silence, I led the congregation slowly, specifically and audibly in an act of repentance, based upon Revelation 3.14–21.

Then it seemed that what we had done verbally, we needed to do visibly. I asked the senior church officials, and my colleagues on the staff, to come with me to every significant part of the church, in order to 'induct' Christ as Head of the Church. Those who were present that night will remember that as we began, at the communion table, I could not continue, and someone had to lead in prayer. Waves of emotion just swept over me – exactly what they meant only the Lord knows, but five or six years later the question I had been asked that Saturday night was being answered that Wednesday evening. Don't try to copy my experience. (God deals with us each in the way that is right for us.)

We can learn from the testimony of others. Mine may help you. Certainly the examples and prayers of confession in the Bible – and especially in the Old Testament – will repay reading and study. But when there is such blessing, why do we so often take so long to respond to the Lord?

Chapter Nine: Notes

1. Kenneth Hagin, *Right and Wrong Thinking* (Faith Library) p. 24.
2. Kenneth Hagin, *How to Turn your Faith Loose* (Faith Library) p. 17.
3. Graham Scroggie, *Method in Prayer* (Pickering & Inglis, 1955) p. 36.
4. The Book of Common Prayer. Confession from Morning and Evening Prayer.
5. *Lancelot Andrewes and his Private Devotions* (Baker Book House, 1981).

Ten: Intercession – The Vital Link

'Intercession is more than just praying for other people!' When I first heard those words I wasn't sure the speaker was right, but as I respected the speaker, I couldn't dismiss the remark. It made me think – what is the real meaning of intercession? You could liken intercession to focusing prayer on a specific situation for others. Just as you can focus the rays of the sun with a magnifying glass onto a particular area of the ground, so you can focus the power of God with the aid of intercessory prayer onto a definite need.

The meaning of intercession

Put very simply, intercession is praying *for* and *against* situations.

(a) *Praying for* In 1 Timothy 2.1–4 Paul urges 'that supplications, prayers, intercessions, and thanksgiving be made for all men, for kings and all who are in high positions, that we may lead a quiet and peaceable life, godly and respectful in every way. This is good, and it is acceptable in the sight of God our Saviour, who desires all men to be saved and to come to the knowledge of the truth.' The very purpose of God is the salvation of the world in a peaceful society, and for those two ends to be fulfilled, the apostle urges that the men – note the *men* – should give themselves to a ministry of prayer and intercession. It has been said that behind the great movements of God in the world have been great intercessors.

We have reason to believe that all great movements of the Spirit of God have had their origin in this prayer agony.[1] Behind the heroes of Christendom – like David Brainerd, Charles Finney, D. L. Moody, and, to come up to date, men like Dr Billy Graham and Luis Palau – were the men and women of prayer, praying for their country and their friends.

We must never divide our praying to God for people, and our witness to people for God. Paul was constantly seeking the prayers of his friends and the young churches that he would be able to grasp the God-given evangelistic opportunities; that he would clearly, boldly and simply preach the gospel; that hearts might be opened to the truth, and that new-born Christians might become strong in their faith. The present stress upon prayer in our churches and for the land should be resulting, among other things, in more and more men and women coming to a faith in God.

Probably the earliest example of intercession for a place and a people was that of Abraham praying for Sodom – that wicked city – Genesis 18. Abraham graciously pleads with God. If there are 40, will you save Sodom? – Yes! What about 35? – Yes! and 30? – Yes! and 20? – Yes? – Yes!

Dr Graham Scroggie, writing about *Methods in Prayer*, says that in intercession 'arms reach upwards towards the throne of grace and outward towards the ends of the earth.'[2] There is a vast range of needs, people, work and places that we can bring to the Lord of Heaven and Earth in this strategic ministry.

(b) *Praying against* That may at first seem unchristian and unfair. But, remember, we are called in Ephesians 6 to wrestle in the spiritual battle *against* all the wiles and works of Satan. The Psalmist did the same thing. 'Contend, O LORD, with those who contend with me; fight *against* those who fight against me' (Ps. 35.1).

Whether we are praying 'for' or 'against' some situation we are not trying to change God. God doesn't and cannot change. Prayer changes us, and others, and challenges the work and grip Satan may have on a situation. For example, we may be praying for a loved one to come to faith in Christ. We may need to pray against the grip that Satan has on them in blinding their eyes to the truth of Jesus. We can pray that they will see the real issues and use of freedom that God has given to them to respond willingly to Christ.

Intercession is also very practical. It is helpful to write down what we have prayed for, and to record the ways and times of God answering. Leonard LeSourd, the husband of Catherine Marshall, records their practical experience in this way: 'In the weeks that followed I filled pages of my notebook, recording the essence of our prayers by date. Our adventure with intercessory prayer had begun, only we didn't label it that way. I doubt if Catherine and I used the term 'intercession' five times during the first twenty years of our marriage. Yet God answered our prayers for others day after day, month after month, year after year. It was all recorded in my notebook.'[3]

Examples of intercession – Moses

Moses was someone who prayed for people in need and also against an evil situation. In Exodus chapter 32 we read that the Children of Israel had disobeyed the Lord, and had foolishly made the Golden Calf. When Moses came down the mountain after his time alone with God, he was horrified at what had taken place. Moses did two things. That same day he called the people to a new commitment to the Lord (26, RSV). The next day he told them that they had 'committed a great sin. But I will go up to the LORD, perhaps I can make atonement for your sin' (30). When Moses returned to the Lord, this is how he prayed (31): 'Oh, what a great sin these people have committed! They have made themselves gods of gold. But now, please forgive their sin – but if not, then blot me out of the book you have written.' Moses was praying *against* the sin of his people, because it was a most grievous sin against God Himself. He was also praying *for* the restoration and forgiveness of the people themselves. For Moses, intercession meant praying for and praying against at the same time.

Examples of intercession – Jesus

John 17 records for us what is often called Jesus' High Priestly prayer, His prayer after the Last Supper. In interceding before the Father, Jesus prayed for three groups of people, and for three purposes.

Firstly, He prayed for himself that God would glorify Him. (That is, strictly speaking, petition. Petition is asking for ourselves. It involves two people: God and me. Intercession, on the other hand, involves at least three people: God, me and the people/person I'm praying for.)

Secondly, Jesus prayed (9) for 'those you have given me'. For Jesus that meant His disciples – those who were near and dear to Him. For us to pray for those whom God has given us will mean our families and friends, those we work with in the office or the Christian ministry, the person we share a flat with. Think of all the people on the inner circle of your life and see them as those whom God wants you to intercede for. The need is that they might be sanctified – that is, that they might be kept free from sin and made pure. How lovely to be able to pray for our children, friends, family etc. at school, work, those who are married and those looking forward to marriage, that they may know the purity of Jesus in all their relationships.

Thirdly, Jesus prayed (20) 'not for those alone. I pray also for those who will believe in me through their message.' There is the wider world where the Church and Christians are to have an influential and effective witness. The world in which we live, the neighbours we have, the missionary work we support, etc. Jesus longs (21) that they may be united in a divided world. There couldn't be anything more relevant than that, could there? Unity between employee and employer, between black and white, Catholic and Protestant.

The examples of both Moses and Jesus will help us understand more clearly the meaning of intercession.

The foundation for intercession

All of us are called to this vital ministry of praying for others because Jesus has made every born-again Christian an intercessor! The New Testament doesn't use that exact word, rather it speaks of us being kings and priests before God.

> 'As you come to Him, the living stone – rejected by men but chosen by God and precious to him – you also, like living stones, are being built into a spiritual house to be a *holy priesthood*, offering spiritual sacrifices acceptable to God through Jesus Christ. . . . You are a chosen people, *a royal priesthood*, a holy nation, a people belonging to God, that you may declare the praises of him who called you out of darkness into his wonderful light' (1 Pet. 2.5, 9).

Peter is picking up a phrase – a kingdom of priests – that first appeared in Exodus 19.6.

Right from the beginning of time it was God's purpose that we should all have the right of direct access to Him. This was God's plan 'A'. Then sin entered the world, and God had to put plan 'B' into operation. Through the ministry and intercession of Jesus, God restored us to the previous position of plan 'A'. God is looking for Christians to fulfil this ministry of intercession.

For example, way back in the Old Testament (Isa. 59.16) 'God saw that there was no-one, and he was appalled that there was no-one to intercede; so His own arm worked salvation for Him, and His righteousness sustained Him.' Or in Isaiah 62.6–7 is written: 'I have posted watchmen on your walls, O Jerusalem; they will never be silent day or night. You who call on the LORD give yourselves no rest, and give him no rest till he establishes Jerusalem and makes her the praise of the earth.'

It was my privilege to be Prayer Chairman for Luis Palau's Mission to London in 1984, and it was that verse in Isaiah 62 which Luis Palau mentioned constantly in encouraging the Christians of London and Britain to intercede for the Mission. 'We were to take no rest, and we were to give the Lord no rest.' We were to take upon ourselves the ministry and burden of praying for the people of London – that they might come to have a personal faith in Christ.

Exactly one hundred years before, Dr Andrew Murray wrote: 'God needs, greatly needs, priests who can draw near to Him who live in His presence and by their intercession draw down the blessings of His grace on others, and the world needs, greatly needs, priests who will bear the burden of the perishing ones and intercede on their behalf.'[4]

Many of us find the work of intercession too hard or seemingly complicated so we do not get involved. Some of us don't see the need for intercession and we do not get involved. Yet it was the Lord Jesus who explained intercession very simply in the parable he told the disciples about the friend coming in need to another friend at midnight. 'And he said to them, "Which of you who has a friend who will go to him at midnight and say to him, 'Friend, lend me three loaves; for a friend of mine has arrived on a journey, and I have nothing to set before him'; And he will answer from within, 'Do not bother me; the door is now shut, and my children are with me in bed; I cannot get out and give you anything'? I tell you, though he will not get up and give him anything because he is his friend, yet because of his importunity he will rise and give him whatever he needs. And I tell you, ask and it will be given; seek and you will find; knock, and it will be opened to you. For every one who asks receives, and to him who seeks finds, and to him who knocks it will be opened" ' (Luke 11.5–8 RSV).

Jesus is simply saying that there is a friend in need. There is a friend who can meet that need. And there is a friend who can bring the two together. The friend in need can be likened to the world and its need. The friend who has the supplies may be likened to God and His limitless resources. The friend who can bring the world in touch with God is the Church – the interceding Christians. Whenever that does not happen the Lord's resources are left untapped, and the world's needs are left unsatisfied.

Partners in intercession

What blessing results when we take up the challenge of intercession, and it is a challenge that we do not have to face alone. Help and inspiration is at hand.

(i) Firstly, in the person of the *Lord Jesus Christ himself*.

If I may put it reverently, what do you think Jesus is doing now as you read these words? Hebrews 7.24–25 tells us the answer – 'Because Jesus lives for ever, he has a permanent priesthood. Therefore He is able to save completely those who come to God through Him, because He always lives to intercede for them.' Jesus' ministry now in heaven is just as important as His ministry on earth and His death upon the Cross. They are complementary. They are the two sides of the same coin of salvation. Dr J. G. S. S. Thomson writes of Christ's intercession and help in this way: 'To lose sight of Christ exalted forever is to lose the consciousness of His presence, His power, and His peace in our hearts, and to lose the secret of victorious living. It is this Lord Jesus Christ, who, from the throne, sends His Holy Spirit upon the Church, and exalts the Church on earth to sit with Him in the heavenlies, and gives her access to all the spiritual blessings that are in Him, and so enables her to live in the power of His own victorious life.'[5]

Imagine, for a moment, that a complete generating power-station has broken down and there is no electricity at all. You could not have a fire, cook a meal, use your electric razor, or heat your hair curlers! To restore all the power that you need, three things have to happen; the central fault has to be put right; the power has to be constantly available, and you need to plug into the power supply for every need you have. It is no use having the supply without using it, nor having a need without the supply to meet it. When Jesus died on the Cross He restored the main supply. Through His intercession in Heaven. He maintains the supply, and by our intercession we plug into that spiritual supply and we and others feel the benefit.

(ii) The second help available to us in intercession is the ministry of the *Holy Spirit*. I have written more fully about this in chapter Four. Let me remind you, however, of God's promise in Romans 8.26–27.

> 'In the same way, the Spirit helps us in our weakness. We do not know what we ought to pray, but the Spirit himself intercedes for us with groans that words cannot express. And he who searches our hearts knows the mind of the Spirit, because the Spirit intercedes for the saints in accordance with God's will.'

In our weakness the Spirit helps. Our weakness may be a disinclination to prayer. It may be difficulty in trusting God to answer what we are praying. It may be ignorance as to what to pray – especially if we are not able to have a full understanding of the need. The Spirit of God will warm our hearts, and pour God's love in. He will direct us to a particular promise in the Bible on which to rest our faith; He will urge or prompt or burden us along particular lines when we do not know how to pray.

A missionary friend of mine had to come home from South America with his family for hospital treatment because of illness. At the same time, the Society he belonged to was seeking a new staff member at home to work among and encourage young people. Before we had really understood that missionary's future, God had prompted Christians in Peru, in London and elsewhere to consider him for this new post. Four months later that is exactly what happened. In our weakness, the Holy Spirit made His purpose very clear.

(iii) Thirdly, we are given *human partners* in the work of intercession. Much of the material for this book was first used with a group of ladies from different churches on a Friday morning in Woodford. Before the meeting two or three ladies would arrive early, to pray for God's blessing, put out the chairs and make the coffee. Every Friday morning before the talk I found myself utterly dependent upon the Lord. I wouldn't have worried if there had been no coffee and we could cope if there were no chairs and we had to sit on the floor, but I would have hated there to be no prayer behind the meeting, and I'm enormously grateful for that human partnership of intercession.

We were reminded earlier (chapter One, page 15) of the way prayer was the deciding factor in the leadership of Joshua. On that occasion, Joshua was grateful for the prayer partnership of Moses, Aaron and Hur. Moses was also grateful for the partnership in intercession with Aaron and Hur, for when he became weary – as we so often do in prayer – he had the support of Aaron and Hur. As a result Moses prayed Joshua through to a decisive victory over the Amalakites down in the valley of Rephidim below.

There are some Christians who have problems with the whole idea of uniting for prayer. They will not be found very often at the church prayer meeting. But where there are human partners perseverance is encouraged, faith is strengthened and our vision is widened. There is a power and a partnership in intercession that is God-given. Take Matthew 18.18–20 for example:

> 'I tell you the truth (says Jesus) whatever you bind on earth will be bound in heaven, and whatever you loose on earth will be loosed in heaven. Again, I tell you that if two of you on earth agree about anything you ask for it will be done for you by my Father in Heaven. For where two or three come together in my name, there am I with them.'

Or, as Professor Hallesby has written:

> 'The greatest transmission of power takes place through the believer's prayers and intercessions. Believing prayer is unquestionably the means by which God, in the quickest way, would be able to give to the world those saving powers from the realm of eternity which are necessary before Christ can return and His kingdom be ushered in. When will the Church of God awaken to her responsibility? In prayer the Church has received power to rule the world. The Church is always the little flock. But if it would unite on its knees, it would dominate world politics – from the prayer room.'[6]

The work of intercession

The clearest example of the work of intercession is found in Isaiah 53.12: 'Therefore I will give him a portion among the great, and he will divide the spoils with the strong, because he poured out his life unto death, and was numbered with the transgressors. For he bore the sin of many, and made intercession for the transgressors.'

Intercession, for the Lord Jesus, entailed four things:

(i) He had to be *identified* with others – the transgressors – those in need.

Jesus is completely different and separate from us. He is the Saviour and we are the sinners. He is the Shepherd, who laid down His life, and we are the sheep who wander away. Yet, though He is different, He is utterly identified with us, in that He became a man like us – except without sin. He was baptised by John the Baptist to identify himself with sinners. He was supremely identified with us in that He bore the sin of the world. Identified in His birth, His baptism, and in the bearing of our sin.

(ii) Secondly, intercession for the Lord Jesus meant that He *bore the burden* for others. He bore the burden of human sin. We can bear the burden of human need. A mother came one day to Jesus and cried out to Him to heal and save her daughter (Matt. 15). Jesus appeared to be hard-hearted and indifferent. The mother pleaded more fervently, and when He saw her faith, Jesus healed her daughter who was about to die. That mother clearly carried a burden. One of the differences between 'praying for' someone and 'interceding' for them is that intercession involves us bearing a burden. We feel the need deeply and persistently. Being burdened means that we do not just mention the situation to the Lord in passing and then forget about it, but we continue in prayer until the answer comes. Since the 1960s and 1970s God has been raising up men and women who are willing to be burdened for and identified with the needs of our nation, through ministries such as Intercessors for Britain,[7] and the Lydia Fellowship.[8] Those who pray for the missionary work of the church also bring their burden to the Lord in intercession. Such saints of the church do not just pray through names on a prayer list. They understand the situation the missionary is facing – the loneliness, the heat, the problems with the language, the toughness of the work, the shortage of money, the weakness that comes from some illness, the tensions that can arise in a small team of missionaries or nationals. Identified with them, such men and women bring the burden of the work before the Lord in prayer as though they themselves were working out in that country and church situation.

(iii) Thirdly, intercession for Jesus demanded a *holy life*. When the writer to the Hebrews contrasts the work of the earthly priests with the ministry of the Lord Jesus as our Great High Priest, he points to the power of Jesus' sinless life. 'How much more, then, will the blood of Christ, who through the eternal Spirit offered himself unblemished to God, cleanse our consciences from acts that lead to death, so that we may serve the living God' (Heb. 9.14). Jesus can make eternal intercession because He is sinless. 'Unlike the other high priests, he does not need to offer sacrifices day after day, first for his own sins, and then for the sins of the people. He sacrificed for their sins once for all when he offered himself' (Heb. 7.27). We shall only be as effective in intercession as our lives are clean and open to the Spirit of God.

(iv) Fourthly, intercession is *costly*. I hope that all I have written so far brings out this aspect. The cost for Jesus is made abundantly clear in Isaiah 53.4–5 RSV: 'He has borne our griefs and carried our sorrows; yet we esteemed him stricken, smitten by God, and afflicted. But he was wounded for our transgressions, he was bruised for our iniquities.' The cost for Jesus was identification with us, and momentary separation from the Father. His work is unique, the cost is unique. But there is still a cost for us. For example, when Paul spoke of his work of intercession in Colossians chapters 1 and 2, he wrote: 'I want you to know how greatly I strive for you and for those at Laodicea and for all those who have not seen my face' (2.1, RSV). It was costly in time, in imagination, in discipline, maybe in fasting, but it was immensely rewarding and a very great privilege. Intercession has been described as 'Love on its knees'. True love never complains, and it is essential that we recapture the value and the strategic importance of intercession in the life of the church. Andrew Murray has written: 'God rules the world and His church through the prayers of His people. That God should have made the extension of His Kingdom to such a large extent dependent on the faithfulness of His people and prayer is a stupendous mystery and yet an absolute certainty.'[9]

How do you react to this work of intercession? Do you feel unworthy? Overwhelmed? Honoured? Daunted? Let me tell you that the ministry of intercession is not the province and privilege of just a few saints who have passed certain exams lower down in the school of prayer. Intercession is the privilege of the youngest Christian, and the most mature saint.

The call to intercession

I have tried, in this chapter, to awaken you to the meaning, value and vital ministry of intercession. I have tried to show you the privileges and the demands of intercession. I want to invite you to join forces with Christians around the world – watched by the saints throughout the ages who have been men and women of prayer – to engage in this work of intercession.

Let me quote Dr Andrew Murray once more:

> 'Most churches think their members are gathered into one simply to take care of and build up each other. They know not that God rules the world by the prayers of His saints, that prayer is the power by which Satan is conquered, that by prayer the Church on earth has at its disposal the powers of the heavenly world. They

do not remember that Jesus has, by His promise, consecrated every assembly in His name to be a Gate of Heaven, where His presence is to be felt, and His Power experienced in the Father fulfilling their desires.'[10]

You and I are priests and kings whom Christ has entitled to exercise such a ministry of intercession. The world needs that ministry. God waits for that ministry. It is in our hands and hearts to enter into it. What a ministry, what a privilege and what a high calling is given to you and me. I pray God will not be disappointed when He looks upon His church and enquires whether we are fulfilling this essential work of intercession[11]. May it not be true of you and me that 'God saw there was no-one to intercede.'

Chapter Ten: Notes

1. Graham Scroggie, *Method in Prayer* (Pickering & Inglis, 1955) p. 67.
2. ibid., p. 60.
3. Leonard LeSourd, *Decision* (April 1985) – *Adventures in Intercessory Prayer*, p. 15.
4. Andrew Murray, *With Christ in the School of Prayer* (Nisbet, 1902) p. 245.
5. J. G. S. S. Thomson, *The Praying Christ* (Inter-Varsity Fellowship, 1948) p. 105.
6. O. Hallesby, *Prayer* (Inter-Varsity Fellowship, 1948) p. 123.
7. Intercessors for Britain. For further information write to: 16 Orchard Road, Moreton, Merseyside.
8. The Lydia Fellowship. For further information write to: 121 Davey Drive, Brighton, Sussex. BN1 7BF. (The Fellowship has some very helpful leaflets on various aspects of prayer which are being increasingly used in local churches.)
9. Andrew Murray, op. cit., p. 116.
10. ibid.
11. World Literature Crusade publishes helpful material on intercession. For further information write to: 320 Hampstead Road, Handsworth, Birmingham B20 2RA.

Eleven: Listening – The Other Side of Prayer

Alongside men like John Bunyan, John Milton and Richard Baxter – great poets and hymn writers of the seventeenth century – stands George Herbert. He came from a family of nine brothers and sisters. His father was related to the Earl of Pembroke who lived at Wilton House, near Salisbury. George Herbert was educated at Trinity College, Cambridge, became a university lecturer by the time he was twenty-six, and shortly afterwards entered Parliament. Suddenly all the advantages of life and privilege seemed to fall away from him. His influential friends died or were disgraced. His mother died. He became ill and suffered much depression, and struggled with a constant sense of his own unworthiness.

However, the pressures and tensions of life taught him one great lesson – the value of listening to God. He would discipline himself to become still and listen. Each time he heard the Lord's voice, so he was strengthened again to face the future. Depression gave way to delight in the Lord, and panic to praise. He became the writer of hymns we sing today such as 'Teach me, my God and King, in all things thee to see', 'King of Glory, King of Peace, I will love thee' and 'Let all the world in every corner sing'.

He learned the lesson of 'Listening' the hard way.

For most of us the world is a noisy bustling place with little time to stop and think, and even less time to listen. We well understand the tension that faced Martha and Mary when they knew that Jesus was coming to stay with them (Luke 10.38–42). 'Martha opened her home to him (Jesus). She had a sister called Mary, who sat at the Lord's feet listening to what he said. But Martha was distracted by all the preparations that had to be made. She came to him and asked, "Lord, don't you care that my sister has left me to do the work by myself? Tell her to help me!" "Martha, Martha," the Lord answered, "you are worried and upset about many things, but only one thing is needed. Mary has chosen what is better, and it will not be taken away from her".'

The text seems to suggest that before Jesus arrived both Martha and Mary had been busy getting ready. Mary hadn't left Martha to do it all by herself. However, when Jesus arrived Mary chose to sit and listen, while Martha was distracted by all around her. The Greek means that Martha's mind was being pulled in different directions at the same time. It is as if, to bring the example up-to-date, the kettle is about to boil over, the children demand attention, there is a caller at the front door, and then the telephone bell rings, and we don't know what to do first. That was Martha. She believed that, though it was desirable to sit and listen, it was just not possible.

The need to listen

The Bible, and especially the Old Testament, stresses that the need to listen is not only desirable, but essential to our spiritual well-being.

If there is one prophet in the Old Testament who knew how vital it was to listen to God – it was Jeremiah. I can almost hear him saying or writing constantly to God's people: 'Listen, listen, listen, won't you!' It is a major theme and appeal running through the Book of Jeremiah. (See for example: 5.21; 6.17–19, 13.10–17; 17.20; 19.15; 20.5; 23.18–22; 29.19–20; 35.17; 36.31.) Perhaps three verses that sum it all up are chapter 23, verses 18, 21 and 22:

'But which of them (the prophets) has stood in the

counsel of the LORD to see and to hear His word. Who has listened and heard His word? . . . I did not send these prophets, yet they have run with their message; I did not speak to them, yet they have prophesied. But if they had stood in my council, they would have proclaimed my words to my people and would have turned them from their evil ways and from their evil deeds.

Someone who had learned to listen to the Lord was young Samuel. As a small child, he had been set free to minister and help Eli, the Priest, in the work of the Temple. It was at the quietest time of the night – just before the dawn broke – that the Lord spoke to Samuel. At first he didn't realise what was happening, but Eli, for all his failings, taught Samuel to say, when God spoke again, 'Speak Lord for thy servant heareth.' God not only spoke to Samuel and showed him all that He would do in the future, but he gave Samuel the faithfulness to pass on to Eli the difficult message received (1 Sam. 3.9–11). It has been said 'For one soul that exclaims: "Speak, Lord, for thy servant heareth", there are ten that say, "Hear, Lord, for thy servant speaketh!" '[1]

It is our privilege, as Christians, not only to speak to the Lord, but also to listen to Him. Jesus taught that He was the Good Shepherd, and we are His sheep. 'The sheep listen to His voice. He calls His own sheep by name and leads them out . . . his sheep follow Him because they know His voice' (John 10.3–4).

Maybe one of the difficulties that many of us have as Christians is that we just do not know how or where the Lord is leading us because we have not heard His voice. We have not learned to listen. Until we have listened, we shall, in fact, not be able to speak effectively.

Children learn to speak because they have first learned to listen. 'The ear hears a word before it speaks it.' Isaiah refers to this truth when he writes (Isa. 50.4–5): 'The Sovereign LORD has given me an instructed tongue, to know the word that sustains the weary. He wakens me morning by morning, wakens my ear to listen like one being taught. The Sovereign LORD has opened my ears.' Often people become deaf and dumb spiritually. If we do not hear, we shall not be able to speak for God.

So there is a need to 'Be still, and know that I am God' (Psalm 46.10).

Learning to listen

It is one thing to know that God will speak to me; it is another matter to know how to listen. There are three main ways of hearing God's voice that I will share with you: meditation, which is feeding on God's word; contemplation, which is discovering God's worth; and listening, which is understanding God's will.

(i) *Meditation* Joshua is given instructions as he prepares to take over from Moses the huge task of leading God's people into the Promised Land. Even though he had people thronging around him at all times, and great and overwhelming responsibilities he is told: 'Do not let this Book of the Law depart from your mouth; meditate on it day and night, so that you may be careful to do everything written in it. Then you will be prosperous and successful' (Josh. 1.8).

The Psalmist is given the same advice. 'Blessed is the man who does not walk in the counsel of the wicked or stand in the way of sinners or sit in the seat of mockers. But his delight is in the law of the LORD, and on his law he meditates day and night. He is like a tree planted by the streams of water, which yields its fruit in season, and whose leaf does not wither. Whatever he does prospers' (Ps. 1.1–3).

Meditation has been defined as thinking deeply or reflecting. If you want to know how an ordinary Christian gets spiritual strength and moral courage from the printed page of the Bible it is by meditating on it. You reflect on and digest all the truths in a passage of Scripture, and take them into your system.

Meditation is personal, simple, and edifying. It builds up the Christian and glorifies the Lord. The truth that is received by the head and the mind is fed down to the heart. We can meditate on many aspects of the Bible – which is our raw material. It may be on a phrase, a verse, a great theme, or a chapter. It may be on a word like 'Lion', 'Lamb', or 'Light'. Take those three words, for example. Look them up in a Bible concordance, and discover the wealth of scriptural and spiritual truth that God has for us. As we reflect on the Bible, so our thinking becomes more and more 'thinking God's thoughts after Him'.

The Psalmist put it like this: 'I have more insight than all my teachers, for I meditate on your statutes. I have more understanding than the elders, for I obey your precepts' (Ps. 119.99–100). Meditation produces insight, and our obedience results in understanding, which in turn promotes holiness. Thus meditation upon the word of God will lead to personal holiness in the man – or woman – of God. Our daily weighing of God's word will govern our daily walking in God's ways.

David Ray puts it like this:

> 'The purpose of Christian meditation is not withdrawal from the society in which you live and from all the stress, problems, change, time and anxiety you face. Instead, through Christian meditation you are drawn to God and you grow in an awareness of His presence in the very level where you live, work and play. The essential purpose of Christian meditation is to increase your personal awareness of God.'[2]

(ii) *Contemplation – discovering God's worth* Let me share two examples with you. Both of them will enrich our understanding of God's worth and greatness.

God as The Rock

Psalm 62.1, 5 says, 'My soul finds rest in God *alone*; my salvation comes from him. He *alone* is my rock and my salvation. . . Find rest, O my soul, in God *alone*; my hope comes from Him. He *alone* is my rock and my salvation.' Twice the Psalmist repeats that God is a rock, and four times the little word 'alone' is mentioned. A rock can provide welcome shade in the heat of the sun. It can be a means of great joy for children scrambling over it at the sea side. The rock will be a real barrier to the gardener digging his garden. Rocks can be awfully uncomfortable if you are trying to sit on two of them of uneven height! Try sitting astride two or three chairs of different heights at the same time, but let one solid chair take all your weight and you have rest. The Psalmist is contemplating the greatness of God as a rock, and delights in the blessing of being able to put all his faith and weight upon God the rock alone.

The Eagle

The second example comes in Isa. 40.29–31: 'God gives strength to the weary and increases the power of the weak. Even youths grow tired and weary, and young men stumble and fall; but those who hope in the LORD will renew their strength. They will soar on wings like eagles; they will run and not grow weary, they will walk and not be faint.'

There are many fascinating references in the Bible to the eagle. When an eagle wants to teach her young to fly she pushes them out of the nest and then will swoop down underneath and catch them on her pinion wings. God sometimes treats us like that – pushing us seemingly beyond our ability, but then stretching out His everlasting arms beneath us so that we do not fall. Again the eagle, with his amazingly sharp eye, can see his prey from afar, and will swoop down with devastating accuracy and catch it. It cannot escape. We may believe that sin and evil can escape detection by God, but His judgement is unerring.

Here in Isaiah we have a third picture of the eagle. The eagle uses his wings to launch in to the air, but as he flies he seeks out the upward air currents and then rests on them. He uses his wings for that purpose. What a contrast between the Christian who is flapping around engaged in this meeting and that committee, being busy in the Lord's service, and the Christian who determines to discover where the currents of God's spirit are active, and then sets his wings to be borne along by the work of God's spirit!

Contemplation is discovering more about God. We have considered God as the rock, and we have seen something of God's nature through the life of the eagle. Our grasp of God is bigger, our faith is stronger and our worship may well be deep and silent.

When all thy mercies, O my God,
  My rising soul surveys,
Transported with the view, I'm lost
  In wonder, love, and praise.[3]

or

Father of Jesus, love's reward,
  What rapture will it be,
Prostrate before thy throne to lie,
  And gaze and gaze on thee.[4]

We are giving our full attention and concentration to the Lord, and marvelling at His greatness, purity and majesty.

Professor Hallesby has expressed contemplation like this: 'Those we know best we don't need to talk to – we have fellowship with each other.'[5] So it can be with ourselves and with the Lord in prayer. We just sit and enjoy the presence of each other. We are much more likely then to hear the faintest whisper or to notice the gentlest movement of a hand when we give the Lord all our attention.

As an illustration of this, the story is told of Wordsworth and Coleridge spending an evening together. They sat either side of the fireplace on a cold winter's night. The fire blazed in the hearth. Neither spoke the whole evening. They just enjoyed the fellowship of each other's company. 'Thank you for a marvellous evening' was the comment as they parted. But how can I be still before the Lord? Psalm 46 is a Psalm that reflects the confusion, change, chaos and noise in the world around the Psalmist, and right in the middle is the instruction 'Be still, and know that I am God' (verse 10).

Some Christians find the following tip helpful in becoming still. Sit on a firm chair. Sit relaxed but upright, with your feet firmly on the ground and your Bible open on your lap so that you are not slouching. Then consciously begin to breathe quietly and deeply and, as you do so, allow the muscles of your shoulders to relax. As you maintain that attitude of stillness and increasing relaxation say slowly and calmly to yourself such words as 'Be still and know that I am God', or 'Jesus is Lord', or 'Praise you, Jesus'. You will very shortly find that all the tension in your body relaxes and your mind becomes still, enabling you to focus more clearly upon the Lord.

Some Christians may be a little worried at such a practical suggestion, and even feel it is silly or dangerous. Don't Yoga or transcendental meditation teach the same thing? Very definitely 'No'. Yoga or TM are asking us to surrender our minds to concepts and thoughts that are more Buddhist than Christian, whereas what we are doing is opening our minds to the unchanging truths of the Lord Jesus, and we are beginning to worship God with all our mind. Some Christians find that it is helpful to take a familiar verse from a Psalm and read it slowly two or three times in order to focus their attention closely.

A colleague described for me what it meant to her to be still before the Lord. She was visiting a convent, and not feeling especially 'holy', but she said to the Lord, 'Here I am, I will just be me and sit quietly in your presence.' She continued: 'One morning at the Holy Communion service, I was standing with the sisters around the Lord's Table, having just received the bread and wine, when I glanced up at a carving of the Risen Christ, and suddenly was enveloped in the love of God and I was filled with stupendous joy – a joy that lasted, for when I came back home eager to share this joy with a friend I thought would understand, found they only acknowledged me in passing, and I could have felt ignored. But it didn't matter, I knew that I had received a blessing from the Lord.'[6]

(iii) *Listening – how does God speak?* Obviously God speaks through the Scriptures if we will read them. There is no doubt about that. The Bible is the living word of the living God for today. He will also use other ways. It may be a simple check on our spirits – we are not happy about some course of action. It may be another person, it may be a dream or a word of prophecy. Such other means will always be in harmony with the Bible. They will never contradict the Scriptures, and will always be appropriate to the circumstances, but they need to be checked out with mature Christians.

May I share a little from our corporate experience in the church fellowship? We had arrived at a point where we needed to know the Lord's leading for the next twelve – eighteen months. We set aside a special Week of Prayer to which reference has already been made. During that week the Lord spoke to us in pictures, through verses of Scripture, through letters from the congregation summing up what they believed God was saying, and then we 'tested' or 'weighed' what was said. We found God was not speaking to us about great building schemes, or massive plans for Christian education and training, but about our attitudes to one another, about the quality of our Christian discipleship, and about the need for us to be turned inside out by the Holy Spirit so that we had a new concern for those who did not know Jesus.

There are other examples to be found in the Bible:

(a) Acts 16.7: 'When they (Paul and his companions) came to the border of Mysia, they tried to enter Bithynia, but the Spirit of Jesus would not allow them to.' We do not know exactly what happened, but Luke seems to suggest that Paul, or one of the companions, was not fully at ease with the plan. Did something crop up to make them have second thoughts? We don't know. What we learn, however, is that when men who are fully committed to God's work and open to His Spirit, suddenly find that one or more of them is not assured of a certain line of action, that may well be God saying 'No' to their plans. They were learning to listen to God.

(b) Colossians 3.15: 'Let the peace of Christ *rule* in your hearts, since as members of one body you were called to peace. And be thankful.' The context is the corporate life of the Christian fellowship. The picture conveyed by the usual Greek word translated as 'rule' is that Christ's peace is like an umpire in a game of tennis. We are familiar with the uncertain line call and linesman's decision. Was a service or a return shot in or out? It is the umpire who decides. In the same way we are not always sure about a decision or a course of action we should take. Do you have peace about it? If you do, and it is according to the written word of God, then God is leading you. You are hearing His voice, and allowing Him to be the umpire.

(c) Paul in 1 Corinthians 12.8 says: 'To one there is given through the Spirit the message of wisdom, to another the message of knowledge by means of the same Spirit.' It is still God's Spirit who is God's agent and messenger, but the means he uses may be different. It may be with a clearly received word or short message or impression that God is speaking to us. When we were beginning a ministry of healing at the church, and we spent time before the evening service asking the Lord to reveal any special needs to which we were to minister, to one person was given the 'impression' that someone would be in church that night with a deep personal problem about which he thought it would be too late to do anything; and that there would also be a visitor in that service who didn't quite know why he was there, but he needed God's help. After that particular evening service, we seemed to have got it all wrong. No one seemed to match the needs God had given us, but we had tried to listen to God in prayer. Two days later someone walked into the church office to explain they had been in church that Sunday night and heard those 'words of knowledge' and knew they must make contact. The caller was the person who felt his needs were too late, and the son with him was the visitor!

(d) 1 Kgs 19.12. 'After the earthquake came a fire, but the LORD was not in the fire. And after the fire came a gentle whisper. When Elijah heard it, he pulled his cloak over his face and went out and stood at the mouth of the cave. Then the voice said to him, "What are you doing here, Elijah?" ' Elijah was facing a time of depression and loneliness after the mighty contest with the Prophets of Baal on Mount Carmel. He needed to hear the Lord again, and God spoke in a gentle whisper. How gracious of God in His dealings with His servant.

And his that gentle voice we hear,
Soft as the breath of even,
That checks each fault, that calms each fear,
And speaks of heaven.[7]

(e) 2 Sam. 12.7 'Then Nathan said to David "You are the man." ' David had grievously sinned and disobeyed the Lord. He had committed adultery with Bathsheba, and murdered her husband Uriah, but God spoke to David through a parable and a prophet. It was direct and simple and clear. 'It's you, David,' God said. God can just as easily shout at us with His word, as He can whisper gently in our ears by His Spirit.

Paul Bilheimer sums up our need to listen to God:

'In order to prepare for usefulness and service, we all need to get into our lives many quiet hours, when we sit alone with Christ in personal communion with Him, listening to His voice, renewing our wasted strength from His fulness, and being transformed in character by looking into His face. Busy men need such quiet periods of spiritual communion, for their days of toil and care and struggle tend to wear out the fibre of their spiritual life and exhaust their inner strength. Earnest women need such silent times, for there are many things in their daily and household and social lives to exhaust their supplies of grace. The care of the children, the very routine of their home life, the thousand little things that try their patience, vex their spirits and tend to break their calm, all of these make it imperative that every Christian woman gets into her life at least one quiet hour every day when, like Mary, she can wait at the feet of Jesus and have her own soul calmed and fed. Too many of us give God only the fag-end of our day.'[8]

Some problems in hearing

We need to listen. God will speak to us. Why do so many of us find it hard to hear what God wants to tell us? Because there are difficulties. They can be summed up in three ways. They are the problems of drawing near to God before we begin to listen; the problem of being distracted by many things as we seek to listen to God; and the problem of disobeying once we have heard what God has said to us.

(i) *Drawing near to God* 'Submit yourselves, then, to God. Resist the devil and he will flee from you. Come near to God and he will come near to you' (James 4.7–8). One of the most marvellous pictures of two people drawing near to each other is told in the story of the Prodigal Son, as returning son and watching father see each other at a distance and run towards one another.

That is how it is with us and God. As we draw near to God, so God is already drawing near to us. Just as the Prodigal Son had to turn an act of will into action and resist all the temptations to delay or change his mind, so when we draw near to God in prayer, we do so as an act of *will*. Not because prayer is a duty, or because we will have an unhappy conscience and feeling of guilt if we do not do so, but because we know from experience the great blessing of that unhurried time with the Lord. We want to draw near to Him. We need to resist all the distractions and disinclinations that Satan would put in our way. As we draw near we may need to quieten our minds and hearts from all that has been going on; we may need to come with confession on our lips; and a prayer that the Lord will make us more and more aware of Him, and help us to magnify Him. We have to learn the importance of drawing near and making vital contact with the living God.

One aspect of drawing near to God relates to the quality of our listening. 'You can listen in order to reply, or you can listen simply in order to hear. Listening in order to reply is what we do constantly. Often, in fact, we only listen, more intent on thinking about our reply.'[9] Dr Paul Tournier expresses the listening problem for many of us – we have not yet learned to give God our undivided attention, due so often to the fact that our hearts and minds face so many distractions.

The same point is made for us by the grandmother of a former United States President – Richard Nixon. 'What thee must understand, Richard, is that the purpose of prayer is to listen to God, not to talk to God. The purpose of prayer is not to tell God what thee wants, but to find out from God what He wants from thee.'[10]

(ii) *Dealing with the distractions* All of us have faced distractions when praying. What are they? And how do you deal with them?

Some distractions are actually caused by our not having enough time for prayer. We are aware there are many situations, needs and people we want to pray for, and we try to cover too much in too short a time. We flit distractedly from one topic of prayer to another. Either we must plan for more time for prayer – i.e. plan that the ten minutes becomes twenty or thirty minutes to cover the growing desires and demands of prayer. Or we must plan our praying so that we cover other needs at other times. Don't try to fit a quart of prayer into a pint of time.

Many people find they need to have a pencil and paper with them when they pray, so that the random thought about a meal, or work, or the children can be jotted down, and referred to later, rather than allowed to lodge in their minds when they are trying to pray. The distraction may also reveal a pressing demand for prayer, and you shouldn't dismiss it. It is a cry for help, so turn that wandering thought into a prayer. 'Stop being a worrier, and start being a warrior'[11] in prayer.

We may find we are distracted when praying because we have chosen a bad time for prayer so far as other members of the family are concerned – they rightly need our attention, and we are having problems because we could have prayed at a time that was better for them, and therefore for us.

The telephone can be a real problem, unless you literally take the receiver off in order not to be distracted when you come before the King of kings.

Jesus knew that His disciples would be distracted, and so he taught them: 'When you pray, go into your room, close the door, and pray to your Father who is unseen. Then your Father, who sees what is done in secret will reward you' (Matt. 6.6). The Eastern society of Jesus' day was a very open air society and the doors would be open wide. Only at night or if people did not wish to be interrupted would the doors be shut. So Jesus is teaching His followers that if they long to be shut in with their heavenly Father, they must learn literally to shut out all that would distract.

(iii) *The problem of disobedience* Now we are at the heart of why we find it hard to hear God. The heart of the problem is the problem of the heart. The Psalmist knew about it (Psa. 95.7–8), the writer to the Hebrews did (Heb. 3.12–19), and the Lord Jesus spoke about it. Quoting from the prophet Isaiah, Jesus said:

> 'You will be ever hearing but never understanding;
> You will be ever seeing but never perceiving.
> For this people's heart has become calloused;
> They hardly hear with their ears, and they have closed their eyes.
> Otherwise they might see with their eyes,
> hear with their ears,
> Understand with their hearts and turn, and I would heal them.'
>
> (Matthew 13.14–15).

If we have a heart unwilling to hear what God has to say to us when we listen, then we may well find that God does not waste His time speaking to us!

An example – Simeon

One man who certainly had not hardened his heart and who was ready and willing to hear God was Simeon. (Luke 2.25–35). His name actually means listening. Simeon walked closely with God. He knew when to respond to the gentlest prompting of the Holy Spirit. He was a man who determined to live a holy life, free from sin. Simeon, we are told, was waiting for Israel to be saved. He was waiting for God to act. He was looking, waiting and expecting God to act. And God spoke – both by His Spirit and through the Scriptures. God was able to reveal to Simeon more of His saving purposes for both Jew and Gentile, the blessings and the demand that Jesus would bring.

God will speak

There is no doubt whatsoever that God speaks and wants to speak to His people – individually and together – today, just as He did in Bible times.

'He who has an ear, let him hear what the Spirit says to the churches' (Revelation 2.7 etc.). The Lord is looking for those who have ears to hear. Elijah, Moses, Samuel and many others in the Bible were great listeners to God and so became great leaders for God. Their lives were changed because they listened to God before they acted for God. As Samuel Chadwick has put it: 'It would revolutionise the lives of most men if they were shut in with God in some secret place for half an hour a day.'[12]

Maybe like Martha, we are pulled in different directions at the same time and have become people of stress and strain, rather than following the example of Mary who knew how to take time out to sit at Jesus' feet and listen to Him.

Chapter Eleven: Notes

1. Pamela Gray, quoted at 'Change the World School of Prayer'.
2. David Ray, *The Art of Christian Meditation* (Tyndale House, 1977) p. 18.
3. Joseph Addison (1672–1719), 'When all thy mercies.' In *Hymns of Faith* 359.
4. Frederick William Faber (1814–63), 'My God, how wonderful Thou art.' In *Hymns of Faith* 11.
5. O. Hallesby, *Prayer* (Inter-Varsity Fellowship, 1948) p. 116.
6. Joan Hicks in a personal note to me.
7. Harriet Auber (1773–1862), 'Our blest Redeemer.' In *Hymns of Faith* 251.
8. Paul Bilheimer, *Overcome through the Cross* (Kingsway, Eastbourne, 1982) p. 93.
9. Paul Tournier, *The Gift of Feeling* (SCM Press 1981) p. 103.

10. Charles Colson, *Born Again*, (Hodder & Stoughton, London, 1976) p. 200.
11. Faith Forster speaking at 'Pray for London' Rally, Royal Albert Hall, January 1985.
12. Samuel Chadwick, *The Path of Prayer* (Hodder & Stoughton, 1931) p. 26.

Twelve: Glorify Thy Name in all the World

Let me retrace for you the journey we have taken. We began by glimpsing something of prayer's potential. We saw it was the deciding factor in changing people. We shared the three secrets about prayer: it must be to the Father, in the name of the Lord Jesus, and in the power and influence of the Holy Spirit.

We have noticed that all along the pathway are those enemies of prayer – the world, the flesh and the devil – that would try to get us off course, or turn us back, or make the going as difficult and sticky as possible. They need not succeed in their purpose because God has given us all the help we need. We can open our hearts in praise to the wonder and greatness of the Lord. Confession will keep us in a right and healthy relationship with the Lord. We have those periods of silence and reading so that we might listen to the Lord and hear His voice and direction and encouragement on the way, and we can come to Him with intercessions on behalf of our fellow believers and the world. As we travel the pathway of prayer, where is our journey heading? Graham Kendrick expresses something of what lies ahead:

There's a sound on the wind like a victory song,
Listen now, let it rest on your soul,
It's a song that I learned from a heavenly king,
It's a song of a battle royal,
Come on Heaven's children,
The city is in sight,

There will be no sadness
On the other side. . . .[1]

It is almost as if we see the glory of the Lord in heaven. We shall do one day. We shall see God face to face and behold His glorious beauty, amazing loveliness and awful purity and fall down in wonder, love and praise before Him. Until that time comes, we still want God to be glorified. Father, glorify your name in all the world. 'For yours is the Kingdom and the power and the glory for ever and ever.'

The reason why Jesus prayed – the Father's glory

The Lord Jesus consistently worked, prayed and lived so that the Father might be glorified. The motive for His prayer and the pattern of His ministry was that God might be glorified. That was His purpose, and that is to be ours also.

Running like a ribbon through His life is this golden thread of glory. It is John who records it so clearly for us in his Gospel.

> 'I am not seeking glory for myself; but there is one that seeks it, and he is the judge (8.50).'

> 'This sickness (Lazarus' illness) will not end in death. No, it is for God's glory so that God's Son may be glorified through it (11.4).'

> 'Did I not tell you that if you believed, you would see the glory of God (11.40)?'

> 'Father, the time has come. Glorify your Son, that your Son may glorify you. . . . I have brought you glory on earth by completing the work you gave me to do. And now, Father, glorify me in your presence with the glory I had with you before the world began (17.1,4–5).'

May we reflect a little more upon what it meant for Jesus to seek only the glory of the Father? When He heard the news that His friend Lazarus, the brother of Martha and Mary, was seriously ill, Jesus didn't go at once to visit him at Bethany. Now, presumably Martha and Mary had sent the news in order that Jesus would come. He didn't. He is acting out this principle 'for the glory of God'. You can imagine how Martha with her perfectionist spirit and slightly critical attitude would have reacted. 'Doesn't Jesus, after all, care? Don't we matter to Him? What's more important – them or us?' And so she would go on and on at Mary. Poor Mary. Poor Martha! Her purpose was to have Lazarus better. Jesus' view was to bring glory to the Father by raising Lazarus from the tomb, rather than the sick-bed. Things would get worse before they got better, and most of us find that hard to accept. We feel that God, if He is to be glorified, should step in at once in answer to our prayers. But experience tells us that this is not always so.

The reason the Early Church prayed – The Father's glory

The apostle Paul grasped that the early church was so to live and work that God was glorified. 'May the God who gives endurance and encouragement give you a spirit of unity among yourselves as you follow Christ Jesus, so that with one heart and mouth you may glorify the God and Father of our Lord Jesus Christ' (Romans 15.5–6).

'Now to Him who is able to do immeasurably more than all we ask or imagine, according to His power that is at work within us, to him be glory in the church and in Christ Jesus throughout all generations, for ever and ever! Amen' (Eph. 3.20–21).

Do you grasp what Paul is after? God revealed and reflected His glory – His very self – in the Lord Jesus. Now he is asking that the Church will also reveal and reflect His glory!!! By the 'church' the apostle means the body of Christ, not the building but the people – whether they worship in the cathedral, or the mission hall, the chapel, school building, front room or the parish church!

The reason why we pray – the Father's glory?

Any Christian leader – let alone any Christian – will often be faced with situations where God does not seem to care about our needs and where He does not answer our prayers at once. We may need new leaders for one particular part of the children's work, or someone to take over running a Bible Study Group, and as hard as we pray, no answer seems to come. Sometimes God waits because He wants us to have the right person for the work, and not just someone to fill the gap. He has promised to answer, but He may delay the reply because He wants to prevent us using prayer solely as a means of solving a problem. Or He may wait so that we do not fall into the temptation of thinking we are good or clever or special in that every time we have a need, we pray and God answers at once. We are not to seek glory for ourselves and God has clearly said that He will not give His glory to another.

It is not unknown for Christian workers to try – even subconsciously – to get in on the act, and allow some of God's reflected glory to shine on them.

We have already noted how Elijah faced that temptation as he challenged the prophets and leaders of Baal, at Mount Carmel, to demonstrate who was the living God. 'The god who answers by fire – He is God' (1 Kgs. 18.24). God only answered when Elijah stopped praying: "O LORD, God of Abraham, Isaac and Israel, let it be known today that you are God in Israel and that I am your servant and have done all these things at your command." and began to pray: "Answer me, O LORD, answer me, so that these people will know that you, O LORD, are God and that you are turning their hearts back again" (1 Kgs. 18.36–37).

Very few of us will be free from the temptation to fear

for our reputation, in the church, or work or wherever it may be, if prayer is not answered. If we appear to fail in our duty, we feel that God has got to act to help us. No, He isn't bound to do that at all. He will act for the glory of His name and not our convenience.

Let me ask you some questions. Why are you praying for a friend or a member of the family to come to faith in Jesus? Is it so that they will be a happier person, or that your life will be easier, or is it so that God will be praised? Our motives may be mixed. We may find elements of all three reasons in our hearts. What God is looking for is that He will be glorified whatever else happens.

Why are we praying that a grandson will succeed at an interview for a job? Is it because the job is just right for him, it is well paid, has good prospects, will bring credit to the home, will open the door to opportunities of Christian service? Or that God might be glorified?

Why are we praying that a fellow Christian or even our minister finds freedom and help from a difficult personal problem or conflict? For their sake, our sake, or the Lord's sake and glory?

Most of us will find it very hard to be absolutely pure and honest in our motives, and often it is right that we do have a mixture of reasons when praying. The point I want to make is that among those motives the glory of the Lord must be pre-eminent. As John the Baptist put it, when he consistently pointed people away from himself and to the Lord Jesus: 'He must become greater, I must become less' or as the old King James Version puts it: 'He must increase, but I must decrease' (John 3. 30).

One person in Jesus' ministry who had not yet learned that lesson was the unnamed mother of James and John, the two apostles, sons of Zebedee. It is Matthew who tells us how she came one day, with her sons, to Jesus, and kneeling down asked if they might sit one on Jesus' right hand and the other at Jesus' left hand in His kingdom. ' "You don't know what you are asking,"

Jesus said to them. "Can you drink the cup I am going to drink?" ' (Matt. 20.22).

This is one of those very human episodes that tells us so much. What was she really asking Jesus? Was it the privilege and honour of being next to Him, or the desire to remain in very close fellowship with Him, or was it a remark that tried to express how great Jesus was, and thus the priceless honour of being with Him? The motives, in asking, may well have been mixed. In His reply Jesus teaches one essential truth, that there is a price to pay if we would glorify Jesus.

The price to pay – the Cross

It is John, one of the sons involved in that incident, who understood what Jesus meant, for he spotlights the glory of Jesus and the cost to the Saviour – and the cost to the disciples, if we would know it.

Jesus realised that the price He had to pay for His Father to be glorified was the price of the Cross. ' "Whoever serves me must follow me; and where I am, my servant also will be. My Father will honour the one who serves me. Now my heart is troubled, and what shall I say? . . ." "Father, glorify your name." . . . "But I, when I am lifted up from the earth, will draw all men to myself." He said this to show what kind of death He was going to die" ' (John 12.26–33).

As Jesus anticipated His coming death, and prayed His great High Priestly Prayer (John 17.1ff), he prayed: 'Father, the time has come. Glorify your Son, that your Son may glorify you.'

Paul has captured the same truth in that marvellous passage in Philippians 2.6–11 . . . '(Jesus) He humbled himself and became obedient to death – even death on a cross! Wherefore God exalted him to the highest place and gave Him the name that is above every name, that at the name of Jesus every knee should bow, in heaven and on earth and under the earth, and every tongue confess that Jesus Christ is Lord, to the glory of God the Father.'

The price to pay – conflict with Satan

The price of glory is not only the Cross, but a conflict with Satan. At the Last Supper, after Jesus had warned that one of the disciples would betray Him, they all began to ask who it would be. ' "It is the one," replied Jesus, "to whom I will give this piece of bread when I have dipped it in the dish." ' Jesus gave the bread to Judas. 'As soon as Judas took the bread, Satan entered into him. . . . Judas went out. And it was night' (John 13.26, 30). Dark outside in the sky, and dark inside in Judas' soul. Once he had gone, Jesus said 'Now is the Son of Man glorified and God is glorified in Him. If God is glorified in Him, God will glorify the Son in himself, and will glorify Him at once' (John 13.31–32).

The price to pay – obedience

We cannot escape the principle that Glory has a price. The price for the Lord Jesus was the Cross, and the price for the believer is obedience: 'If you love me, you will obey what I command.' 'If anyone loves me, he will obey my teaching.' 'He who does not love me will not obey my teaching' (John 14.15, 23–24). Isaiah put it this way in Chapter 26: 'O Lord, our God, other lords besides you have ruled over us, but your name alone do we honour' (13).

'Obedience is the path of power in prayer. The baptism of the spirit, the manifestation of the Son, the indwelling of the Father, the abiding in Christ's love, the privilege of His Holy Friendship, and the power of all-prevailing prayer all wait for the obedient.'[2]

The cost of obedience

Christian obedience is a very personal and practical response. First of all, for many of us, it will affect our use of time and that is something we all feel we are short of when it comes to prayer. If we really want the Lord glorified, then we shall put other things to one side, and ensure that prayer has its right time. One of the clearest examples of what this meant in practice is that of David Wilkerson. We have already seen that once he decided to switch off the television set in the late hours and use the time instead for prayer, then God began to use him. Here was a man who meant business with God, and God responded to him. Most of us will find it is a constant battle to find time, to make time, to take time out of our lives and daily programme in order to pray. No one is going to give that time to us, and Satan is certainly going to try and steal time from us, cause us to waste it, fritter it away, and even when we have managed to get time to have it interrupted in one way or another. None of us will be free from that battle, but it is a battle we can win.

Secondly, we shall face misunderstanding. It may be within the family – why spend time praying? We may face it within the local church – why stress the prayer meeting, and spend much time with the people who pray, and not with others? People will misunderstand why, if we include prayer within our worship services, we also choose to meet for prayer before the service. They may misunderstand why we need to meet together to pray, when we can just as well pray about a need at home on our own. Once you begin to mean business with God about prayer, you will face misunderstanding.

Thirdly, misunderstanding may lead to mockery. For some it may be the gentle mockery of being described as a 'member of the God-squad'! But it is interesting to discover that often the very people who have mocked when all is well, have turned to 'the God-squad' and asked for prayer when there is a special need.

If mockery is experienced before or after times of prayer then, fourthly, real attacks of depression may be experienced both during and after prayer. Depression is one of Satan's weapons that he fashions and uses against those who want to take prayer seriously. Don't misunderstand me. I am not suggesting that a great deal of depression is the result of prayer. Nor, that when we pray, we should expect to face depression – just the opposite. What I am saying is that depression is one of the weapons that Satan appears to be using against Christians in the spiritual battle.

A willingness to face – and be exposed to – the spiritual battle is the last practical aspect of the cost I will mention. Paul has warned us about this in Ephesians 6.2: 'Our struggle is not against flesh and blood, but against . . . spiritual forces of evil.' We have already seen that the battle is real, that the weapons we need have been provided, and that the battle can and will be won through the victorious Name of Jesus. But there are few churches and Christians willing to pay the price of victory.

Obedience results in blessing

Because Jesus was willing and able to pay the cost of bringing glory to the Father through the Cross, the history of the world, and the salvation of every person has been completely changed. I believe we also would find great changes taking place if the church in the twentieth century around the world was willing to pay the cost of praying and working solely for the glory of God.

If the cost seems too great just consider the results that follow when Christians have been willing to pay it – results in our own lives, in the church, and in the world.

The results in our own lives

One of my favourite passages in John's Gospel is in chapter 7.37–39: 'On the last and greatest day of the Feast, Jesus stood and said in a loud voice, "If any man is thirsty, let him come to me and drink. Whoever believes in me, as the Scripture has said, streams of living water will flow from within him." By this he meant the Spirit, whom those who believed in him were later to receive. Up to that time the Spirit had not been given, since Jesus had not yet been glorified.' Just as the Holy Spirit was given in His fulness to the church at Pentecost (once Jesus had been glorified by His death and resurrection), so we will know the power and ministry of the Holy Spirit in His fulness as we glorify the Lord Jesus in our lives. He will be like a stream of living water flowing out to the dry and thirsty areas around, bringing life and refreshment and hope. Not only will others be refreshed, but every believer constantly going on thirsting and going on coming to Christ, and going on drinking, will find the Spirit going on flowing out. As Jesus is glorified, then our own spiritual lives are greatly blessed.

The results in the Church

Later in John's Gospel, Jesus used the Old Testament picture of the vine (see Isaiah 5, and Psalm 80). He had come as the True Vine, and the disciples were to abide in Him, so that the life of Jesus could flow into and bear fruit in each disciple, as a branch bears the fruit. As Jesus says to His disciples (John 15.8): 'This is to my Father's glory, that you bear much fruit, showing yourselves to be my disciples.' Various fruit is mentioned in this section: effective prayer, genuine discipleship, an awareness of the love of Christ, the fulness of joy in our hearts, a loving fellowship, and a knowledge of Jesus, not as servants to a Master, but as friends to a Friend. What a contrast this list is with so much of our church life with its ineffective prayer, lukewarm Christianity, uncertainty of Christ's love, lack of joy, tension and division in the congregation, and the sense that God is remote. What makes the difference? The desire that God and Christ alone should be glorified. Once the motive is right, then God can begin to make us as He longs we should be.

The results in the world

God's glory is not just to be found in the Christian and the Church, but also in the world. It was into the world that God came as the Word became flesh. 'Full of grace and truth; we have beheld His glory, glory as of the only Son from the Father.' (John 1.14, RSV). God desires to go on showing forth His glory through His word in the world. Jesus has told us (John 14.12–13) 'I tell you the truth, anyone who has faith in me will do what I have been doing. He will do even greater things than these, because I am going to the Father. And I will do whatever you ask in my name so that the Son may bring glory to the Father.' Jesus came into the world for the salvation of men and women. He came to bring wholeness (for that is the meaning of salvation). He came to defeat sin, and Satan and sickness through His death and resurrection. He came – and His Church comes – to bring the words and the works of salvation to people around the world. Wholeness of our relationship with God in Christ, wholeness of mind and body and spirit. Christ came to announce – and the church comes to continue – the work of bringing the good news of the kingdom and reign of God.

It is not we ourselves who have to do all this. It is God who does it in and through us. It is the Spirit, flowing out from the heart of the Christian, who longs that Jesus should be glorified. It is Christ who bears the fruit in our lives as we abide in Him. It is God the Father who does these works in and through us (1 Thess. 5.24). God, Father, Son and Spirit, works in and through us. We have found a new perspective. No longer are we thinking and talking about what we can do for God. Rather we talk of what God will do for us. The perspective has changed, because the motive has changed. Now we can sing and pray: 'In my life, Lord, be glorified. . . . In my home, Lord, be glorified. . . . In my work, Lord, be glorified. . . . In your church, Lord, be glorified. . . .'[3]

The motive for prayer has changed – now we long for God's glory. Because the motive has changed, prayer will change people. Prayer will change people because God changes people.

Chapter Twelve: Notes

1. Graham Kendrick, Thank you Music 1979. In *Mission Praise* 235. Used with permission.
2. Andrew Murray, *With Christ in the School of Prayer* (Nisbet, 1902) p. 181.
3. Bob Kilpatrick, Prism Tree Music. In *Mission Praise* 105. Used with permission.

Discussion Questions

A few churches have used the book for group study and discussion. The following questions – some suggested by Sue Penfold of St. John's, Buckhurst Hill – might encourage others to do the same.

Chapter 1. Prayer is the deciding factor in many areas of life (See James 4.2–3; 5.16). Yet, most Christians find prayer hard. In what ways do *you* find prayer difficult? What help in prayer are you hoping to find in reading the rest of the book? Make a list – you'll need it later!

Chapter 2. If God is our Father, then we are His children. What difference can this relationship make to our praying? Because of past experiences some people find it very hard to visualise God as their loving Heavenly Father – how could the group help a Christian in this situation?

Chapter 3. 'In Jesus' Name, Amen' – it's a common way to end prayers, but what does it mean? Is it just a conventional ending like putting 'yours faithfully' at the bottom of a letter? Or, does it have a deeper significance? (See John 14.12–15; 15.14–17 and 16.22–24). What kind of prayers could you *not* pray 'In Jesus' Name'?

Chapter 4. Praying in the Spirit is not an optional extra available to only a few Christians. We are *all* commanded to pray in the Spirit (Eph 6.18) – see page 48ff and 56ff for the meaning. The Holy Spirit helps us in our weakness (Rom 8.26). In what ways are you weak in prayer? Make a list and then see from the Bible references in this chapter how the Holy Spirit can make you strong.

Chapter 5. 'The world either undermines our prayer or is undergirded by our prayer'. Therefore: In what ways are we guilty of thinking that practical action is more important than prayer – either in our church life or personally? How can we answer the criticism that praying can be an excuse for not getting on with things ourselves?

Chapter 6. 'The Spirit is willing, but the flesh is weak'. This sums up, for most of us, the problems in prayer. Seven practical steps are outlined in this chapter to help us overcome the self-centredness of prayer. What step do you personally – or the group corporately – need to work on first, and what specific action should you take to find that prayer changes people?

Chapter 7. Make a list of all the tactics the group thinks Satan uses against you. (If you want ideas see pp. 96–98). From which verses in the New Testament can we be sure that Satan has been defeated? (See p. 94). We have been given God's armour to help us win the battle (Eph 6.10–18). How can each piece of the armour help you foil each of the tactics you have listed?

Chapter 8. Read Psalm 95.1–7 and list all the reasons given here for praising the Lord – what additional reasons can the group suggest? Try to imagine what your life would be like if you never praised the Lord – what would you be missing? How can we incorporate praise more effectively into our Sunday worship and our daily lives? (A hint: Stop worrying about all you have to do today, and begin to offer it all to God as worship. You will find it makes a difference.)

Chapter 9. Is it right to include the following prayers of Peter – Luke 5.8; Matt 16.16; John 21.15 and Acts 3.6 as prayers of confession? In what ways do they all differ?
Imagine that a friend comes to you who has hit rock-bottom spiritually. They feel they have let God down so badly that they can not continue as a Christian. What help can you give to them? (Use Peter's experience and also David's in Psalm 51.)

Chapter 10. How would the group members define 'Intercession'? Compare your answers with pp. 132ff and 142ff.
Most Christians find intercession difficult. Are there practical steps the group can suggest to help each other in this aspect of prayer? What aspects of local, national or international affairs do you need to be praying for at the present time?

Chapter 11. Prayer is a two-way relationship with God, but is it so in reality? Why do you find it so difficult to listen to God? How do you expect to hear God speaking to you? Reflect upon Luke 10.38–42 for some answers.

Chapter 12. What practical difference has reading this book made to your personal and group prayer life? Why? Why not?
You made a list – at chapter 1 – of the help in prayer you hoped to get from your discussions, how many of your hopes have been realised?